THE SPIRAL OF TIME SERIES

RAV DOVBER PINSON

THE MONTHS
of TAMUZ and AV

vol **5**

EMBRACING BROKENNESS
TRANSFORMING DARKNESS

IYYUN
PUBLISHING

IYYUN PUBLISHING

Published by IYYUN Publishing
232 Bergen Street
Brooklyn, NY 11217

http:/www.iyyun.com

Iyyun Publishing books may be purchased for educational, business or sales promotional use. For information please contact: contact@IYYUN.com

Editor: Reb Matisyahu Brown

Developmental Editor: Reb Eden Pearlstein

Proofreading: Alyssa Elbogen

Proofreading / Editing: Simcha Finkelstein

Cover and book design: RP Design and Development

Cover image: by Rochel Shiffrin
© 2015 Deuteronomy Press, used with publisher's permission as a gift to the Iyyun Center.
See **www.circlecalendar.com** for more information.

pb ISBN 978-0-9914720-8-6

Pinson, DovBer 1971-
The Months of Tamuz & Av: Embracing Brokenness, Transforming Darkness
1.Judaism 2. Jewish Spirituality 3. General Spirituality

vol **5**

THE MONTHS
of TAMUZ *and* AV

EMBRACING BROKENNESS
TRANSFORMING DARKNESS

17TH OF TAMUZ | TISHA B'AV | TU B'AV

IYYUN PUBLISHING

THE MONTH OF TAMUZ

DEDICATED IN HONOR & IN THE MERIT OF
THE NESHAMA OF

נרשון חנוך נ״ע

GREGG HENRI ROBIN

May his Neshama have an aliya and may the publication
of this Sefer bring to us the time when those who lie
in dust will awaken and sing in joy.

THE MONTH OF AV

DEDICATED IN HONOR & IN THE MERIT OF

DR. ALEXANDRA SHUSTINA שתחי׳

Bracha and Hatzlacha.
In the merit of Blessings and Success in all areas of her life.
May she see the fulfillment of all her heart's desires.

And Dedicated to
GERSHON (GREGG) AND CHANI BELL שיחי׳
AND THEIR CHILDREN
IN THE MERIT OF GOOD HEALTH AND SUCCESS.
and
YAAKOV ELKAN AND ORLI ELKAN שיחי׳
FOR THEIR CONTINUED SUPPORT TO THIS PROJECT.

CONTENTS

ॐ

OPENING

*E*ACH MONTH OF THE YEAR RADIATES WITH A DISTINCT quality and provides unique opportunities for personal growth
and illumination. Accordingly, every month has a slightly
different climate and represents a particular stage in the "story of
the year" as expressed through the annual cycles of nature. The
winter months call for practices and pursuits that are different than
those of the summer months. Some months are filled with holidays
and some have only one or none. Each month therefore has its own
natural and spiritual signature.

According to the deeper levels of the Torah, each month's distinct qualities, opportunities and natural phenomena correspond
to a certain set of data arranged within a 12-part symbolic structure. The spiritual nature of each month is therefore articulated
according to its unique entries for each of the 12 data points which

include: 1) a permutation of G-d's Four-Letter Name, 2) a verse from the Torah, 3) a letter of the Aleph Beis, 4) the name of the month itself, 5) an experiential "sense", 6) a Zodiac sign, 7) a tribe of Israel, 8) a body part, 9) an element, 10) a unit of successive Torah portions that are read during the month, 11) a season of the year and 12) the holidays that occur during the month.

By reflecting on these twelve themes and categories, an ever-ascending spiral of insight, understanding and practical action becomes revealed. Learning to navigate and harness the nature of change, and being truly engaged with the cycles of time, adds a deeper sense of purpose and heightened presence to our lives.

The present volume will delve into the spiritual nature of the summer months of Tamuz and Av according to these 12 categories. It is important to note that this is a different structure than what is usually employed for the books in the Spiral of Time series. In every other book, the focus is on a single month. However, for reasons which will become clear to the reader as they progress through the text, the months of Tamuz and Av are explored as an integral unit. This will allow the reader to get a more wide-angle view of the archetypal energies and processes that are active during the course of these two unique summer months.

NOTE: *For a more comprehensive treatment of this 12-part system and the overarching dynamics of the "story of the year," an in-depth introduction has been provided in Volume One of this series, The Spiral of Time: Unraveling the Yearly Cycle.*

PART I:

ॐ

The Month of Tamuz

TRANSFORMING NEGATIVITY
THROUGH POSITIVE VISION

HE MONTH OF TAMUZ CONTAINS THE LONGEST AND some of the hottest days of the year. The natural world is a perfect reflection of the spiritual world; in other words, the physical mirrors the spiritual. Thus, if the biosphere (considered for our purposes from the perspective of the northern hemisphere, which includes the Land of Israel), boils with intense and uncomfortable heat in Tamuz, it reflects the fact that this is spiritually the 'harshest' time of the year as well. This physical revelation of spiritual 'harshness' can be a source of stress, chaos, destruction, and dysfunction.

Tamuz is understood as the month in which the beginning of all 'destruction' occurs, it is thus the 'headquarters' of deviance and decay, as it were. A time-honored spiritual response to destruction is to fast, whether communally or individually. In *TaNaCh* / Torah, Prophetic and Scriptural Writings, Tamuz is a month explicitly related to fasting (*Zecharyah*, 8:19) — meaning that not only are particular days within Tamuz connected with fasting, but that each of its days are appropriate for fasting (*Minchas Chinuch*, Mitzvah 370). The month as a whole is thus understood as a spiritually dangerous time in which one must be extra cautious and conscious of the ramifications of their actions.

From an inner perspective, the heat of Tamuz also contains the potential for powerful transformation, positive heat and illuminating light. Naturally, physical heat fosters emotional heat, which can intensify a desire for purely physical gratification. On the other hand, we always have the choice and the ability to elevate a base desire to its root within the spiritual dimension, where all is truly beneficial. This rerouting and rerooting of desire and its psycho-behavioral ripple effects is a primary focus of our spiritual work during the month of Tamuz.

Hot weather makes people want to expose more of their body, even if only in a modest way. People also tend to socialize more in the summer than in the winter. They go out with friends, meet new people, and travel to new places. This greater exposure and interaction can exacerbate sensual desires, especially in those who have not refined their way of seeing and relating to others, as will be explored.

Desire and jealousy both correspond to the summer months of Tamuz and Av respectively. When desire is aroused, so is its companion, jealousy. When a person's eyes see what does not belong to him, his heart may nonetheless desire it. When people cannot receive or achieve what they desire, they can become jealous, envious and even full of rage. Therefore, when the heat of summer sets in, we must work to integrate the potentially harsh energies of Tamuz properly in order to remain free from harmful desire, jealousy and anger.

Eyes are the source of desire, and thus jealousy. "We desire only what we see" (*Sotah*, 8a). What we want and desire is dependent on the things we observe. "Hashem says, if you give me your eyes and heart, I will know that you are Mine" (*Yerushalmi*, Berachos, 1:5). The eyes are the filters that bring both conscious and subliminal information into our system. In the month of Tamuz, we need to work on rectifying our eyes — to counteract negative tendencies and cultivate positive vision, in order to see without jealousy. This will allow us to begin to create a *Tikkun* / healing and repair for our desires; a process which will be further engaged during the following month of Av.

Moving from Spring into Summer:

Throughout the preceding three months of spring, we experience a progression of personal, psychological and spiritual evolution. The first month, Nisan, evokes gratitude and humility with the reception of the unearned gift of miraculous freedom. Hashem took us out of slavery by the scruff of our neck, as it were, with a strong arm and outstretched hand. We did nothing to attain our freedom other than submit to the word and will of Hashem. In this way, we become conscious of the presence and power of the Divine 'You' in our lives; the Cosmic Other beyond ourselves whom we may encounter and engage throughout our lives. Accordingly, the work of Nisan is focused on acknowledging and appreciating this 'You' in all its manifestations.

Imbalanced humility, however, can tend toward humiliation and a sense of worthlessness or nihilistic self-nullification. To rectify this imbalance, the second month of spring, Iyyar, inspires the polar opposite manifestation: strong self-expression and a sense of personal will. Through our daily counting of the Omer, we gradually refine our vessels to receive the Infinite Light of Torah. Following the 'awakening from above' that we experience in Nisan, we self-generate an 'awakening from below' during the month of Iyyar in preparation for the revelation of Sinai. Therefore, the month of Iyyar is largely focused on expressing and evolving the 'I'.

The third month of spring, Sivan, helps us harmonize and unify these opposite energies of humility and self-worth — creating a space in which 'you and I can both exist' — illustrated by its astrological sign of *Gemini* / the Twins. The three modes of identity evoked by these three spring months — 'you', 'I', and 'we' — when not properly balanced, can manifest as their respective distorted counterparts:

'You' — jealousy (I am jealous of what *you* have.)

'I' — false desire (*I* want *my* desires to be fulfilled.)

'We' — attachment to honor (I want to give *you* honor, but only in order that *I* will receive honor.)

In the hot summer months of Tamuz, Av, and Elul (loosely corresponding to July, August and September), we have to be especially aware of each of these three forces and work on refining and re-balancing ourselves. In Tamuz we work with *Kin'ah* / jealousy. In the month of Av we work with *Ta'avah* / false desire. In Elul, we deal with *Kavod* / attachment to honor.

This is the general overview of our spiritual development in relation to the turning of the seasons as we move from spring to summer. Now, let's turn our attention to the unique energies and dominant themes of Tamuz as reflected in the 12-point symbolic structure, as discussed above.

☾

֍

PERMUTATION
OF HASHEM'S NAME

HE FOUR LETTER ESSENTIAL NAME, YUD–HEI–VAV–HEI (Hashem), is the Divine Source of all Reality. A linguistic interpretation of the four letters of the Name in correct sequence is as follows. The last three letters of the Name, Hei-Vav-Hei, create the word *Hoveh / is*. The root of this verb means, 'to bring into being'. The first letter of the Name, Yud, serves as a prefix to the last three letters, Hoveh. In this way, the Yud modifies the verb to represent a perpetual activity. In other words, the Divine Name can be understood to mean, 'That Which is Continuously Bringing Being into Being'.

The Essential Name cannot be spoken, therefore a common practice is to rearrange its four letters into an alternate spelling that produces the word HavaYaH, which literally means 'bringing being into being.' This aspect of the Name refers to the Ultimate Being, which is the Source and Substance of all that is. The Ultimate Being does not depend on anything else to exist. It gives rise to all past, present and future manifestations, thereby bringing all things into existence ex nihilo, i.e. *Yesh meAyin* / being from non-being.

There are four letters in the Name of Hashem (Yud-Hei-Vav-Hei). Every month is defined by and connected to a different permutation of these four letters. Each permutation communicates a different spiritual dynamic encoded within the Divine signature of that particular month. As Hashem is the Source of all existence, this name formation is the primary source of the other 11 points of light/information included within each month, and is therefore understood as the spiritual foundation of the entire month. In the month of Tamuz, the letter-sequence is the exact opposite of the 'proper' sequence of Hashem's Name; instead of Yud-Hei and Vav-Hei, it is Hei-Vav and then Hei-Yud.*

---

* The vowels in the sequence of Hashem's Name for the month of Tamuz are: Segol-Hei, Tzeirei-Vav, Cholam-Hei, Chirik-Yud. This month's letter-sequence is taken from the last letters of the verse of the month, where, as the attentive reader will notice, the letters have different vowels than the ones named above. Still, as the *Tikunei Zohar* (Hakdamah 2b) explains, whether we use the first or the last letters of the verse to determine the month's letter permutation, we always use the first letters of the verse to determine the vowels. Therefore, the vowels are Segol-Hei and Tzerei-Vav, etc., even though the letter Hei in the actual verse is 'silent.'

When the letters of Hashem's Name are in their 'proper' sequence, this represents a Divine flow of kindness and open revelation. When the letters go 'backwards,' it represents a constriction and concealment of the Divine flow. In Nisan, for instance, a month of Divine revelation and compassion, all of the letters are in their proper order. Tamuz, by contrast, is a time of extreme Divine concealment and harsh spiritual energy. According to the Zohar, Tamuz is one of the three harshest months, along with Av and Teves (*Zohar* 2, 12a). The Zohar also says that Tamuz belongs completely to Eisav, the 'harsh', unrefined brother of Yaakov. Eisav corresponds to the nation of *Edom* or Rome, which viciously attacked *Yerushalayim* / Jerusalem, our spiritual center, during the month of Tamuz. .

Being that the flow of the Divine Name is completely reversed during this month, Tamuz is a great opportunity to 'turn our lives around', to reverse our negative trends and transform them into positive trajectories. As we heal ourselves, we realign the Divine Name, so to speak, and convert 'concealment' into 'revelation'.

The Arizal also teaches that each of the 12 months of the year are connected with the 12 letters in the Divine name *Adon-oi* / 'my Master'. This name is spelled with four letters: Aleph-Dalet-Nun-Yud. The 'fully expanded spelling' of *Adon-oi* spells out the names of each of these four letters: Aleph is Aleph-Lamed-Pei. Dalet is Dalet-Lamed-Tav. Nun is Nun-Vav-Nun. And Yud is Yud-Vav-Dalet. In total there are 12 letters in this expanded spelling. These 12 letters represent the 12 months of the year. Tamuz is the fourth month of the year, and so it is connected with the letter Dalet. Av is the fifth month of the year and is connected with the letter Lamed.

Dalet and Lamed together spell the word *Dal* / poor. During this season we should meditate on the harshness of our spiritual poverty, and its cause — our lack of self-mastery. This recognition can inspire us to turn ourselves around and become revealers of the Master of the World.

☾

ૐ

TORAH VERSE

HE FOUR LETTER DIVINE NAME THAT SHINES DURING EACH month is rooted within a particular verse in the Torah (*Tikunei Zohar, Hakdamah* 9b. *Eitz Chayim, Sha'ar* 44:7). In other words, there is a 'verse of the month' comprised of a four-word sequence, in which each word either begins or ends with the letters of the *Tziruf* / name-formation for that month. (In fact, the order of the Tziruf follows the corresponding verses. *Mishnas Chasidim*, Meseches Adar, 1:3.) The meaning and context of the verse connected with each particular month is, of course, also part of the revelation of that month's guiding light.

The permutation of the Divine Name that we explored above comes from the last letters of the verse, "*ZeH einenO shoveH liY* / This is worthless to me...." (*Megilas Ester*, 5:13). These are the words of Haman, who wished to annihilate the Jewish people in the Purim story. Haman is the closest advisor to the king, a man of great wealth and high prestige. Everyone in the kingdom of Persia is required to bow to him, and they do, besides one man: Mordechai the Jew. In our verse, Haman is speaking of his extreme jealousy. He has everything he desires, and yet, as Rashi comments, he says: All my honor is worthless to me when I see Mordechai sitting at the King's gate.

This is the sick nature of jealousy — you can own virtually everything in the world, but if you lack one thing that you really want, it feels like you have nothing at all. Haman's *Kin'ah* / jealousy of Mordechai characterizes the covetous quality of Tamuz.

"Jealousy, desire and honor-seeking drive a person from the world" (*Avos* 4:21). These are the three primary emotional misalignments that alienate people from their reality or "world". There is a certain reality that we all live in, consisting of who we are, what we have, where we live, and so forth. When we are jealous of another person, whether jealous of their assumed accomplishments or of their possessions, we are "driven from our world". When this occurs, we no longer reside comfortably in our reality, but become inconsolably restless and unmoored within an illusory world of poverty, disempowerment and perceived insult.*

---

* There is also a productive type of jealousy, although the emotion itself is still 'harsh'. For example, if you are jealous of another person's accomplishments, you may motivate yourself to accomplish more and thereby become more productive to fill your lack (*Baba Basra*, 21a). But jealousy for the sake of being jealous provides no productive motivation or fulfilment whatsoever. This is the type of jealousy that is being discussed in this volume — the unproductive, negative jealousy which in the end only exacerbates one's sense of existential lack.

The same dynamic is at play when dealing with desire. If you unconsciously obey an insatiable desire for other people or things, you will perpetuate the gnawing notion that you can't possibly be content with your life and your world as it is. Similarly, if you are driven to gain *Kavod* / honor, you will never be satisfied, no matter how much honor is bestowed upon you. There will always be at least one person who will detract from your honor or question your greatness — like Mordechai to the honor-crazed Haman. You could be on a high dais speaking to thousands of people who hold onto every wise and poetic word you utter, but if you are an honor-seeker, one little child whispering softly in the back of the room will irritate you. The slightest appearance of disrespect will throw you out of equilibrium and take you out of your world.

Both desire and honor share the paradoxical characteristic that the more you acquire, the more you require. The more one slavishly feeds their desires, the stronger their hunger becomes. The same is true for honor. They are both bottomless pits that can never be filled. Satisfaction and contentment are always just out of reach, as stated succinctly by our Sages: "If you chase honor, honor runs away from you" (*Eiruvin*, 13b).

These three issues — jealousy, desire, and honor-seeking — are the very reasons Adam and *Chavah* / Eve were driven out of *Gan Eden* / Paradise when they ate from the Tree of Knowledge. They were told not to eat from the Tree of Knowledge, but they were also told that they could eat from anything else; literally everything was available to them except this one tree. What, then, enticed them to desire specifically this one tree, and finally to eat from it?

Chavah "saw that the Tree of Knowledge was good for food and pleasing to the eye…, desirable for gaining wisdom; she took some and ate" (*Bereishis*, 3:6). Thus it was *desire*, initiated by the act of seeing, that drove Adam and Chavah to eat. Chavah had told the snake that she must not eat the fruit, as Hashem had prohibited it. The snake cleverly retorted and told her that Hashem said not to eat from the Tree only because "Hashem knows that when you eat from it your eyes will be opened, and you will be like G-d, knowing good and evil" (*Bereishis*, 3:5). Thus, it was also an issue of *honor* and self-aggrandizement, initiated through the act of hearing, that motivated Adam and Chavah in this instance; they were impelled to eat because they wanted to be "like G-d".

Furthermore, according to the Medrash and Zohar, the snake was driven by *jealousy* over Adam's relationship with Chavah, and also over the "garments of light" in which they were bathed. Based on this archetypal series of events — from the snake's jealousy, to Chava's desire and honor-seeking, to Adam's uncritical acceptance of and inability to take responsibility for his actions, resulting in the paradigmatic experience of exile — we can see how intricately these three emotions are interconnected. And it is these three attributes that we will explore and seek to refine over the three months of summer including Tamuz, Av and Elul, respectively.

LETTER

*T*HERE ARE TWENTY-TWO LETTERS IN THE ALEPH BEIS. As the Torah, which is the 'Blueprint of Creation', is written in Hebrew, the *Lashon haKodesh* / Holy Tongue, the Sages teach that each of these twenty-two letters contain a host of metaphysical energies and creative potentials. According to the Sefer Yetzirah, a profound book of early Kabbalah that pays particular attention to the inner dimensions of the Hebrew letters, the twenty-two letters of the Aleph-Beis are divided into three categories: three "Mother Letters", seven "Double Letters" and twelve "Simple Letters". Each month is connected to one of the twelve Simple Letters.[*]

---

[*] For a more in-depth analysis of all three categories of Hebrew letters and their relationship to the calendar, please see the introductory volume in this series: *The Spiral of Time: Unraveling the Yearly Cycle*

The letter of the month is Ches (ח). The graphic design of this letter consists of two walls and a ceiling, but no floor. A floorless letter, say our Sages, represents the potential of falling, as symbolically one can 'fall' through the open bottom of the letter (See *Menachos*, 29b). The letter Ches therefore suggests a spiritual fall and the fear that accompanies such a disorienting experience (*Gittin*, 70a). Ches actually comes from a word meaning fear (*Bereishis*, 35:5. See *Pardes Rimonim*, Shaar 27:11). What's more, the letter Ches (or "*Chet*" in the Sephardic and Middle Eastern pronunciations) sounds like the word *Cheit* / sin or missing the mark (*Shoftim*, 20:16).

The first time the letter Ches appears in the Torah is in the word *Choshech* / darkness: "…and darkness was on the face of the abyss" (*Bereishis*, 1:2).* Darkness is another symbolic reference to spiritual falling. This indicates that the month of Tamuz has an amplified potential for intense spiritual descent, darkness, and destruction. Of course, we must always remember that if we have the ability to destroy, we also have the ability to create. If we can descend, we can also ascend. In fact, Chassidus teaches that at times we descend specifically in order to ascend. In such a case, we may use the momentum gathered from our fall or contraction to catapult us to new heights.

---

* The first time a letter appears in the beginning of a word in the Torah is directly representative of the underlying quality of that particular letter. *Toldos Yitzchok* by a Talmid of Reb Rav Isaac Chover, p. 39b. See also *Bnei Yissachar*, Iyyar, Ma'amar 3. See; *Baba Kamah*, 55a.

Tamuz is connected with the sense of sight, as we will soon explore in greater detail. The first time the Torah speaks of sight is when it says, "...and He (Hashem) *saw* that the Light was good" (*Bereishis*, 1:4). Sight is therefore connected with light. According to the deeper teachings of the Torah, 'darkness' actually refers to a very intense light — so intense that it cannot be revealed, much like a black hole (R. Tzadok, *Pri Tzadik*, Tamuz). This is the *Choshech* of Tamuz; the blinding light so strong that it must necessarily manifest first as darkness. For this reason, Ches is also the number eight, alluding to a redemptive level above and beyond the natural cycle of seven, hinting at the transcendent 'light of darkness' or 'dark light'.

The darkness of Tamuz is expressed most vividly in the catastrophic destructions that happened throughout Jewish history during this month, as we will soon explore. And yet, this is a month of great potential light. For example, the 17th of Tamuz, the very day we mourn the beginning of the destruction of Jerusalem, will one day be transformed from a day of fasting and mourning into a great holiday and celebration of light.

'Darkness' can also refer to a kind of destructive vision or 'dark gaze,' called *Ayin haRa* / evil eye. *'Ayin haRa* is rooted in *Kin'ah* / jealousy, as a person is first jealous of someone and then places an Ayin haRa upon them. In the words of R. Eliezer Azikri, the 16th Century Israeli mystic and poet: "A person who looks upon another person with jealousy causes an Ayin haRa to rest upon the person he is observing" (*Sefer Chareidim*, Divrei Kevushin, 4). In general, as Rabbi Menachem Rikanti (1250-1310 CE) writes: "Know that the sense of sight has power to affect, for good or for ill." (*Rikanti*,

Vayikra, 19:4. See also *Ben Yehoyadah*, Berachos 152a). In the language of Rabbeinu Yonah, "A type of 'toxic vapor' is released from the eyes of a person who has an Ayin haRa, which emanates from within his thoughts and 'burns' what he is looking at" (Rabbeinu Yonah, *Avos*, 2:11. See also, *Derashos HaRan*, Derush 8).

Looking at another person with jealousy releases a negative energy, which obscures the Light of Creation. If this negativity is absorbed by the recipient, it can have a deleterious effect (*Toras Chayim*, Baba Metziya, 84; *Chazon Ish*, Ha'aros Baba Basra, Siman 21). Yet, it is important to note that this 'energy' only has an effect upon one if they 'accept' or 'believe' in its power to do so (R. Yaakov Kaminetzky, *b'Mechitzos Rabbeinu*, p. 229-230). This is a subtle point that we will explore in more depth shortly.

Av, the month following Tamuz, is associated with the letter Tes. Ches and Tes are the two vocalized letters in the word *Cheit* / missing the mark, misalignment or sin. These two months in the heat of the summer are both understood as the harshest and most spiritually dangerous times of the year. Accordingly, both the First and Second Temples in Jerusalem were destroyed over the course of these two months. This shared sense of spiritual harshness and historical distress during Tamuz and Av is what binds these two months into one long process of destruction, initiated by the accumulated negative effects of our collective Cheit.

Yaakov / Jacob, at the end of his life, wanted to reveal the *Keitz* / End Times to his children, the Twelve Tribes of Israel. As soon as he began to speak, however, the *Shechinah* / Divine Presence left him (*Bereishis*, 49:1. *Medrash Rabbah*, Rashi ad loc). As a result, he wondered whether his children had some spiritual blemish that made them unworthy of receiving this revelation. When his children realized this, they said, *Shema Yisrael...* / Hear Israel (our father), Hashem is our G-d, Hashem is One. The Baal haTurim (*ibid*) writes that they also said, "Father, look at the letters of our names and you will notice that within them there is no Ches or Tes. This shows that we are free of *Cheit!*" (*Zohar* 2, 230a). Yaakov was pleased with their response, but he retorted, "Neither is there a Kuf or Tzadik, which spell the word *Keitz* / end (of time), so I cannot reveal to you what will be at the end times." Such information, therefore, needs to remain shrouded in darkness until our consciousness has been refined enough to reveal its Hidden Light for all to see.

The word *Cheit* is spelled Ches-Tes-Aleph (חטא). Aleph, numerically '1', is symbolic of the One True Divinity. Aleph is also a silent letter. This reminds us that the omnipresent One is present even within 'sin,' albeit silently. The deepest truth is that even within 'sin' and darkness, there is a spark of light hiding. There is always the potential for light, meaning and purpose within every life situation; sometimes we just need to look deeper to find and reveal it.

As mentioned, *Ches* is also a word which means 'fear'(*Yechezkel*, 32:32). This month calls upon us all to meet and overcome all our fears and anxieties. When we face our darkness, and really feel our pains, brokenness and sadness, whether it is from what we have done and created, or from what life has dealt us, we can only then begin to transform it all into light. When we can be deeply present with the 'destructions' of our own 'inner temples', instead of anxiously pushing them away and covering them up, we can catalyze the ultimate healing hidden within these seemingly dark months. The clarity and light that emerges from this reflective process is like that which can come after a good cry, as we will explore in more depth shortly.

The graphic design of the letter Ches can be viewed as a Vav (ו) and a Zayin (ז) connected by a small line on top. Vav is the letter of Iyyar, and Zayin is the letter of Sivan. The word Tamuz (spelled Tav-Mem-Vav-Zayin) can be divided into two parts: Tav-Mem which spell the word *Tam* / complete, and Vav-Zayin, which are the corresponding letters (and a code word) for the months of Iyyar and Sivan, the months which directly precede Tamuz. This teaches us that the month of Tamuz can serve as a 'completion' of the previous two months. When we transform our darkness into light, our brokenness into healing, and our sins into merits during the month of Tamuz, we complete the spiritual growth that we began in Iyyar, the time of introspection, and Sivan, when we received the Torah.

NAME OF THE MONTH

ACCORDING TO THE TORAH, NAMES ARE POWERFUL things. Comprised as they are of Hebrew letters, they represent and define the energy or attributes of that which is named. Our names, for instance, unlock and reveal hidden potentials in our own spiritual makeup. Similarly, names of other people, places, and periods of time provide subtle hints as to their deeper purpose or poetic significance. Additionally, changing one's name is akin to a kind of rebirth; some might even say that a change of name initiates a change of *Mazal*.

Each month of the twelve months of the year has a distinct name, and every name has a meaning. According to our Sages, the current names we have for the months were imported to our tradition upon our return to Israel from the Babylonian Exile. They can in fact be traced to ancient Babylonian or Akkadian names (*Yerushalmi*, Rosh Hashanah, 1:2, *Medrash Rabbah*, Bereishis, 48:9). In the times before the Babylonian Exile, the names of the months were mostly known by their number in the sequence of the year. For example, the month of Av was called the Fifth Month, and Cheshvan was known as the Eighth Month.

Before the Babylonian Exile, Tamuz was simply called 'the Fourth Month.' Only after the Exile did it take the name *Tamuz*. In the Torah the word Tamuz is related to the concept of heat, as we find in an etymologically similar word *l'Meizei*, as in "l'Meizei l'Atuna / the furnace heated"(*Daniel*, 3:19). As we have discussed, the heat of Tamuz is related not merely to physical heat, as in the heat of the summer sun, but also to emotional heat and specifically the heat of jealousy. In the month of Tamuz we need to face and refine the fearful, 'hot' emotion of jealousy in order to elevate it and use it to catalyze positive transformation.

Tamuz is actually the name of an idol (or the name of a known idol worshiper) and a pagan practice (*Yechezkel*, 8:14). This idol represented a deity, or a seer of the deity, who was violently killed by his wife, or by a jealous, rival king (Rambam, *Moreh Nevuchim*, 2:29) at the time of the Summer Solstice. It appears from the Prophets that the worshippers of Tamuz would heat the idol with fire to create an illusion of tears. The image of the deity Tamuz was a hollow statue. Lead would be placed in the sockets of its eyes, and when a fire was heated on the bottom of the statue, the lead would slowly melt. As a result, it would appear as if the idol was shedding hot tears, as

Rashi explains (Rashi, *Yechezkel*, 8:14). The dramatic visual effect of the weeping idol inspired the onlookers to similarly wail and cry for their own loss at the end of the summer. This ritual created a kind of collective catharsis of grief.

With the arrival of the Summer Solstice, and the longest day of the year, which often occurs within the Hebrew month of Tamuz, the time of weeping for this idol and its worshippers would commence. Indeed, many ancient civilizations marked the decline in daylight hours, signified by the Summer Solstice, with a period of mourning for their pagan deities. During the ritual weeping of Tamuz, women would gather around the idol and join its 'weeping'. It is explained that they cried because the summer was ending, as it is from the point of the Summer Solstice that the days begin to get shorter.

When the spring comes, people are naturally filled with hope, optimism and the energy of new beginnings. For the isolated, especially those living on farms and villages in the ancient world, the winter months were a time of hibernation. But once the spring came they would be swept up in new hope and fresh growth; women who were alone at this time were filled with dreams of finding love. Now, in Tamuz, as the Solstice had passed, if they were still alone, they would cry for their unrealized hopes and the love that they did not find. These were tears of deep *Yi'ush* / overwhelming despair that lamented the end of hope in the face of the inevitable tragedy of life. They were thus tears of 'death' and *Tum'ah* / closedness, stagnancy or blockage of possibility, which is understood by the Torah as a kind of death or 'impurity'. These were also tears of *Avodah Zarah* / alienating worship, which is centered around a static, rigid, solidified and defined form. This worldview is related to the world of 'fate' — the opposite (l'havdil) of Elokim Chayim, the G-d of Life, which is constantly flowing, fluid and always fresh with new potential.

The idolatrous weeping of Tamuz is obviously connected to the Torah-based custom of mourning and weeping for the beginning of the destruction of the Holy Temples in the month of Tamuz. Yet, there is a monumental difference between these two forms of weeping, and it is vital to understand this. Equipped with this understanding, we can begin to transform subtle forms of idolatry in our own lives, and help clarify the true import of Tamuz for the whole world.

The psychological underpinning and roots of the *Avodah Zarah* and mythology-laden mode of weeping focuses solely on what is lost — the sun, the dream of love, etc. This is the meta-root of theatrical tragedy. Tragedy means that we can aspire to work against fate, but in the end, fate always wins; everything must die and end. Avodah Zarah is intrinsically connected to death, stagnancy, fixity, *Yi'ush* / despair, the feeling of giving up and ultimately, tears of loss.

Obviously, mourning real loss is valid and necessary for human life. However, to avoid the trap of subtle idolatry, our mourning and grief must also be open to the acknowledgment of the Living One, who is the all-powerful Source of Potential Goodness. When we are connected to the Infinite One, we too can overcome 'death' and 'endings' in order to rise again. When we view life from this perspective of infinite potential, our weeping can be an expression of holy and productive yearning for Hashem and for our eventual

Redemption. This produces a grief that is existentially bitter and yet paradoxically hopeful and energizing. This is the crux of the difference between these two types of mourning: Does your weeping signify a surrender to inevitable fate, or do your tears clarify your yearning for a potential Redemption within the midst of your life's ruins?

Weeping for the idol may have been intended as a way to overcome fearful emotions, yet the practice inevitably marred a person's vision of life, causing an increase in alienation, despondency and a heightened sense of anxiety that life will continually become darker and darker. This is *Tum'ah*, the consequence of *Avodah Zarah*, and a purely circular worldview. The Torah's guidance in how to mourn the lost Temples in Jerusalem, however, clarifies our view of life, and helps us cultivate a consciousness full of Divine Light, hope, faith and trust in a redeemed future.

In order to fully understand this subtle distinction, we must realize that there are many types of tears, including tears of despair, tears of longing, tears of *Atzvus* / despondency and tears of *Merirus* / bitterness. In the idol worship of Tamuz, the women cried over a false belief in the fixed end of fate, which initiated a relinquishment of hope. The weeping deity died or was killed, and is crying at the summer solstice for the death of the summer, representing a death of hope for future growth and giving rise to a general sense of despair in the face of the tragic nature of life. The transformation and elevation of this paradigm is to weep with an openness to hope, to experience one's tears of grief as redemptive tears of longing and trust in a new day. When we mourn the destruction and loss of our Beis haMikdash — our spiritual center and Hashem's chosen portal for open revelation in the world — we must sensitize ourselves to the great pain of this ongoing tragedy. However, we must be simultaneously filled with hope, trust, and longing for the healing of the world, the coming of the Moshiach and the Redemption of love, light and infinite possibility.

Deep down we are bitter, even desperate, over the world's condition of exile. Yet faith empowers us to embrace our sadness and feel the world's pain, without resorting to 'giving up' in despair. To the contrary, because we know that the world once had a Beis haMikdash, we know that it will be so once again, but on an even deeper and higher level than before. Because in the past we experienced redemptions and open revelations, we are certain that one day the whole world will be redeemed, and perfect wholeness will be revealed to all. The very act of longing creates a bridge between that perfect wholeness and our present conditions of suffering. Conscious grieving opens us up to accessing a taste of Redemption, even amid all the brokenness that we experience within ourselves and within the world.

☾

♈

SENSE

*T*HE CONVENTIONAL WORLD IDENTIFIES FIVE SENSES, YET *Sefer Yetzirah* speaks of the *twelve Chushin /* senses. In addition to the more commonly understood definition of what comprises our 'senses', the word *chush* can also mean, 'a sensitive level of perception, understanding, appreciation and skill' in relation to a particular psycho-spiritual process or function. For example, a 'sense of sleep' is a deep understanding and appreciation of sleep which includes both: what sleep represents spiritually, as well as the practical skills and abilities that make one's experience of sleep both peaceful and beneficial.

These twelve *Chushim* are also the twelve activities that the Torah describes the Creator performing in the perpetual process of maintaining the world (*Pirush haRavad, Sefer Yetzirah*). As we are created in the Divine image we also possess all twelve *Chushim*, at least in potential.* Every month gives us the ability and strength to expand our vessels (potentials) for a particular *Chush*, along with its corresponding Divine Attributes. When we align and refine our consciousness via these *Chushim*, we can harness the qualities of each month in a most profound and meaningful way.

The month of Tamuz is associated with the sense of sight. *Yirah* / seeing is spelled exactly the same as the word *Yirah* / fear or awe. As we discussed above in connection with the letter *Ches*, the concept of fear is intimately related to the harsh energy of this month. Indeed, fear is often a primary motivator to avoid or protect oneself from impending suffering or harm. During the summer, it is therefore important for us to protect our eyes, not only from the harsh ultraviolet rays of the sun, but most importantly from negativity and immodesty, which lead to jealousy or harsh judgment. By guarding our eyes and exercising choice in where we direct our vision, we can protect ourselves from the harsh *Din* / judgment present in this month.

The first time the Torah mentions 'sight,' it is with regards to the Light of Creation: "Hashem saw the Light and it was good." When sight is unpolluted by jealousy, it is a very spiritual sense,

*Even if one is blind, for example, he always has the *potential* for sight — it's just that he is currently missing the physical vessels (capacity) for it (*Pirush HaGra, Hakdamah, Sefer Yetzirah*). However, the sense of sight is included in the person's Divine image, as it were. Obviously, a physically blind person could have immense vessels for spiritual sight.

capable even of allowing us to perceive the Hidden Light of Creation. When we are able to see the light in something or someone, we can, like Hashem, declare: 'It is good'. Then, instead of only being affected by what we see, we can also have an effect *upon* what we see. For Hashem, proclaiming the goodness of the Light of Creation was not only acknowledging that which was already present within the Light, but was in effect actually defining its attributes. The Light actually *became good* as a result of Hashem's innate Goodness, which was then channeled through His positive perception and projective expression, as it were. During Tamuz we are invited to see the 'good', even within suffering, and to thereby affect what we see for the good. The Arizal teaches that this is an opportune time to create a Tikkun for our 'eyes'. It is in essence a time to actively cultivate a positive and healthy view of life.

In this month, the *Meraglim* / scouts or spies in the wandering community of Israelites went to "see the Land". On this reconnaissance mission, they traveled through the Holy Land for 40 days, returning back to the community on the Ninth of Av. The bulk of their journey was therefore in Tamuz; they 'saw' the Land during the month of 'seeing', and they reported what they saw back to the people in Av, the month of 'hearing'.

Eyes are extremely sensitive and spiritual tools. Even a speck of dirt causes great physical discomfort in an eye and creates an obstruction of vision. Similarly, even a speck of *Gashmiyus* or 'materialistic focus', let alone jealousy, can obscure the *Ruchniyus* / spirituality of our vision.

The two 'great' sins of man in the Torah, both the eating from the Tree of Knowledge and the creation of the Golden Calf, each began with a skewed sense of sight. The *Cheit* / sin and downfall of Adam and Chavah, began when Chavah "*saw* that the Tree of Knowledge was good for food and pleasing to the eye…she took some and ate" (*Bereishis*, 3:6). The meta-root of the Cheit of eating from the Tree of Knowledge was that "Adam gazed at the place of *Kelipa* / negative energy" (Alter Rebbe, *Torah Ohr*, 6:1. Miteller Rebbe, *Toras Chayim*, 33:1). As a result, they were ejected from the Tree of Life reality. Similarly, the episode of the Golden Calf began when "the people *saw* that Moshe was late coming down the mountain (*Shemos*, 32:1). They 'saw' darkness and confusion, and thought that surely Moshe passed away (*Rashi*, ad loc), and thus they desired to create an image that they could clearly see and serve. In both cases, the people's eyes deceived them from perceiving the truth of reality. As a result, there was, and are, collective consequences that we are still working on repairing to this very day.

When we see people and things deeply and positively, we benefit ourselves as well as those whom we see. To create a Tikkun for our eyes, and return our perception to a positive view of the world, we must see with eyes of *Kedusha* / holiness.

The Art of Seeing

We do not see objects the way they are, but rather the way *we* are (See *Divrei Chaim*, Zos Chanukah: "A man's eyes are connected to his heart." See also, *Avodah Zara*, 28b, Tosefos, *ad loc*. "Eyes follow the heart." *Medrash Tehilim* (also known, as *Medrash Shochar Tov*) Chap 14:1). When we change ourselves, we change the way we view things. On a deeper level, we also change the very things we are viewing.

The world is our mirror. What we see on the outside is a reflection of what is happening inside. If we see ugliness or negativity, it is because we have a trace of ugliness or negativity within ourselves. Likewise, when we see beauty or goodness, it is because we have beauty and goodness within. "Hashem saw the Light, *Ki Tov* / and it was good" (*Bereishis*, 1:4). A literal reading of this verse is, "Hashem saw the Light, because *He* was good." Hashem saw Light and Goodness because Hashem is the Source of all Goodness. We, too, see goodness when we are a source of goodness and see ugliness when we harbor distorted points of view.

Rabbi Eliezer, the son of Rabbi Shimon, was coming from Migdal Gedor, from the house of his teacher. He rode along the riverside on his donkey, and was feeling happy and elevated because he had studied much Torah. There he met an exceedingly ugly man, who greeted him, "Peace be upon you, my master!" Rabbi Eliezer did not return his salutation but instead said to him, "How ugly you are! Are all the people of your city as ugly as you?" "I don't know" replied the man, "Why don't you go to the Craftsman who made me, and tell Him what an ugly vessel He has made?" Realizing that he had seen and spoken wrongly, Rabbi Eliezer dismounted his donkey, prostrated himself before the man, and pleaded, "You're right. Forgive me!" But the man replied, "I cannot forgive you until you go to the Craftsman who made me and tell Him, 'How ugly is the vessel which you have made.'" (*Ta'anis*, 20a-b).

Rabbi Eliezer thought that he was intellectually elevated and spiritually 'perfect', but when he saw ugliness in another he was forced to ask himself: 'Why am *I* seeing this ugliness?' He knew that what we see on the outside is a reflection of our inside. This is why Rabbi Eliezer was disturbed when he realized his mistake. The man responded correctly, saying: 'Hashem created me this way — this is *my* perfection. Perhaps you still need to work on seeing the perfection in everyone, not just in yourself, for if you were truly perfect yourself, you would see perfection everywhere and within everyone.'

The eyes are the only parts of the body that do not appear to change due to aging. If you look at yourself in a mirror, your eyes may look exactly as they did when you were a child. The 'changeless' nature of the eyes suggests that they are windows into the changeless soul of a person. Therefore, in order to see people the way they really are — in order to see the good in them — you should train yourself to look into their eyes and into the changeless soul within. If you look at another this way, without creating discomfort by awkwardly staring at them, they will sense that you are really seeing *them*, not judging them or scrutinizing their superficial appearance or status. This is a way to 'see without personal motive', and a good way to train yourself to perceive people's inherent goodness and spiritual potential. When seeing another in this way you will also get in touch with your own changeless goodness, as they look back into your eyes. Eventually you can train yourself to see the Divine goodness within everyone and everything.

Here is an exercise to develop deep seeing: Two people sit opposite one another and simply look into each other's eyes for a set period of time, whether for one minute, ten minutes, a half hour or even a full hour. Be present with the thoughts and emotions that arise, but return again and again to the intention of looking deeply into the reality of the other. Experience the reality of seeing and being seen. Connect with their inner 'I' through their outer eyes. After some time, write freely about the experience to process any insights gained.

The Process of Vision

What we see 'out there' is a reflection of what is 'in here'; we see things the way *we* are, not the way *they* are in and of themselves. The world is thus a mirror of how we think and feel. But on an even deeper level, *how* we look at things actually affects *what* we see.

Ancient and medieval philosophers argued about how vision works, and gave two major theories:

In order to see something, the light from an object comes toward us and our eyes receive it. The movement is thus from object to subject. Or, alternatively:

Our eyes emit the 'light' of vision, which goes out to meet objects. The movement is thus from subject to object. (For these two opinions, see; R. Meir Aldavia, *Shevilei Emunah*, Nosiv 4, p. 154. Rabbi Gershon Ben Shlomo, *Sha'ar haShamayim*, Ma'amar 9, p. 53. Rabbi Pinchas Eliyahu of

Vilna, *Sefer haBris*, 1, Ma'amar 17:3. Rabbi Tzadok HaKohen of Lublin, *Kometz haMincha*, 2.)

Today, empirical scientific evidence agrees that images of sense-objects are received in your brain. As you look at the words on this page, for example, rays of light pass from the page to your eyes, and these register as an inverted image of the page in your retina. Light-sensitive cells then cause impulses to pass through your optic nerve, leading to complex electrochemical patterns in your brain, which you finally interpret as a page with words on it turned right-side-up. This is a one-way path, from the object to the subject.

Yet, one part of this process still remains a mystery. Why do you see the image of the page as 'outside' of you, while the image is actually appearing within you, or within your brain? If one were perceiving accurately, perhaps it would be more natural to say, "I am seeing a page in my mind," rather than, "I am seeing a page some two feet away from my face." It is only our projection of the image *outward* onto an assumed 'external' world that makes objects appear to be independent and outside of our mind. In this sense, we could argue that we project or 'emit' the light of vision outward. Our minds in some way do extend to the outside world, so-to-speak (*Likutei MoHaRaN*, 1:76. *Bnei Yissachar*, Kislev, Ma'amar 4. *Shem Mishmuel*, Lech Lecha).

Taking this idea further, we enter the arena of basic quantum theory, in which the observer is understood to affect the observed through the very act of observation. Contemporary biologists and theorists discuss another mystery, namely that some people can accurately sense when an unseen person is staring at them. Here, not only does a visible seer affect the seen, but even an invisible seer somewhere 'out there' can seem to affect us 'in here'.

According to the deeper teachings of Torah, the way we see things does indeed affect them in certain ways. When we look at something, we project our own image on the surface of what we are looking at (*Ramban*, Vayikra, 18:19. *Shevilei Emunah, Nosiv haShelishi*. p. 114. *Tzeida laDerech*, Ma'amar 2, Klaal 1:2. *Sichos haRaN*, Chap. 242. See also: *Nishmas Chayim*, Ma'amar 3:4. *Kav haYashar*, Chapter 2). Our vision emits subtle vibrations into the universe and towards the object or person we are viewing. Looking at something with a simple purity of soul creates a positive energy between seer and seen, while looking at something with a distorted or impure quality of soul creates a negative field between seer and seen (*Agrah dePerkah*, Chap. 160, p. 171. *Agrah d'Kalah*, Shemos). Looking at something with good-intentions and good-will emanates goodness and blessing (*Ben Yehoyada*, Shabbos, 152a. *Zohar* 2, 217b). Bad intentions emanate negative vibrations which can actually harm someone who is not protected (*Ya'aros D'vash* 1, Derush 12. *Malbim*, Mishlei, 23:7). We therefore impact what we observe (*Magen Avos* [Tashbatz], Avos, 2:16. Arizal, *Sefer Halikutim*, Parshas Kedoshim).

Our eyes are powerful. This power is a reflection of Hashem: the ultimate creative power of the universe. The 'Name' of the Creator is the Four-Letter Name, the Yud-Hei-Vav-Hei. The four colors of the eyes correspond to these four letters. The outer 'white' of the eye is the transcendent level of *Keser* / crown (or *Chochmah* / Divine wisdom), represented by the letter Yud. The streaks of red and gold-ish colors in the eyes correspond to the upper Hei, the aspect of *Binah* / understanding. The coloring of the iris — such as brown, grey, blue or green — corresponds to the letter Vav, the six emotional Sefiros of *Zeir Anpin*, including *Chesed, Gevurah, Tiferes, Netzach, Hod* and *Yesod*. The almost black color of the pupil corresponds to the final Hei of the Divine Name, represented by Malchus (*Zohar Chadash*, Yisro. *Kav HaYashar*, Chapter 2).

As they mirror the Ultimate creative force of the universe, the Name of Hashem, our eyes have the amazing ability to create, to give life and to reveal goodness and blessing. And yet, within this creative power is also the ability to destroy, to curse and to conceal or remove life.

Moments of Creation & Moments of Destruction

Creation is continuous. Every year, every month, every day, every hour — and really every moment — a brand new revelation of Divine Light enters into the world, revivifying and reanimating the Creation anew. This ever renewing flow of life resonates with a unique, distinct frequency at every moment.

Insofar as each moment is a totally new Creation, it must be that 'in between' each moment there is a total deconstruction and end of the old Creation, allowing for the completely new to emerge. As every moment is a new *Yesh* / existence, then, as a matter of course, between each of these originary moments everything must go back into a state of *Ayin* / no-thingness or non-existence.

Chesed / loving-kindness and giving is the foundation of Creation. The desire of the Creator to create is itself an act of Chesed — to create the very possibility of an 'other' with whom to give and share the gift of life and love.

Yet, if Creation were an expression of Infinite Chesed alone, without any *Gevurah* / restriction, the world couldn't even appear to come into any semblance of separate existence from the One. In other words: without Gevurah, there would be no creation, only the Creator giving wholly of Himself to Himself. Therefore, a necessary byproduct of Gevurah is *Tzimtzum* / contraction and concealment of Hashem's Infinitude. Even if somehow the creative process could occur without Tzimtzum, that finite world would be instantaneously overwhelmed by Infinity. Gevurah and Tzimtzum are thus the river's banks which keep and contain the living waters in their course without swallowing the shore, allowing dry land to exist.

And so, every moment has elements of both revelation and concealment, creation and destruction. There is a continuous pendular movement, a Divine 'exhale' filling the void with *Yeshus* / something-ness, and a Divine 'inhale' withdrawing itself, as it were, and leaving a fertile void in its wake. Every moment has a dimension of Divine Chesed, creating, giving, and expanding into existence — and a dimension of Gevurah, restricting, retracting and nullifying existence. These two movements are the meta-source of our freedom to choose: to give and support life, or (G-d forbid) to take and detract from life.

We all have the ability to create or destroy, to offer love and light, or, Heaven forbid, to spew hatred and darkness. We can give life and we can take life. Give to the world or take from the world; contribute or receive. Protect others and the world or destroy others and the world. We can do so because there are two Divine forces, as it were, at play within the One Field of Being. Of course, both attributes are manifestations of the One actively creating, destroying and maintaining creation. There is the force of Chesed, giving, and the force of Gevurah, restricting and holding back.

The book of *Tehilim* / Psalms speaks about a *Rega* / moment of Divine *Apo* / anger (30:6). In the Torah, we find that Hashem tells Moshe, "If for one single Rega I would go in your midst, I would destroy you" (*Shemos*, 33:5). The *Rega* mentioned here is the moment of Gevurah 'in between' the moments of Creation. This is what can appear as *Apo*; destroying or undoing life.

Our Sages teach us that once a day there is a moment of Divine wrath (*Berachos*, 7a). What does this mean? Could it mean simply that within the cycle of 24 hours there is a single moment, such as every day at 4:44pm, in which the Creator is 'angry'?

Of course, there is a deeper intent behind these prophetically inspired words. When our Sages said there is a moment of Divine wrath within every day, it means that there is a microscopic instant of Gevurah, of holding back, withdrawing, destroying and un-doing, within every moment. This Gevurah is not inherently negative or 'angry' — it is part of the same Divine 'breathing' process that lovingly creates existence on the exhale. However, when we misuse or abuse the instant of Gevurah and concealment, we are capable of harming, cursing, and destroying ourselves and others, Heaven forbid.

The root of the *Sitra Achra* / other side, or *Kelipah* / obscuration of light, is grounded in this recurring 'moment' of Gevurah and Tzimtzum. Acts of *Kelipah* are purposelessly 'negative' and needlessly detract from life, for example: chopping down a tree for no reason, hunting for sport or flippantly insulting another person, for that matter. The actions of a Tzadik consciously tap into the Divine flow of Chesed in order to create and give to others and to the world. When a Tzadik practices Gevurah or withholding, it is only for a greater purpose in ultimately expressing Chesed. The opposite of the Tzadik is the *Rasha* / one who lives for himself alone at the expense of others. The Rasha uses Gevurah to destroy, harm and take away from life, whether on overt or subtle levels.

Every moment of life we have a choice: We can draw down more Chesed into the world, and become co-creators with the Divine Source in bettering and benefitting creation, making this world a true dwelling place of the Holy One. Or we can, G-d forbid, draw down more detrimental Gevurah, and the opposite of life. We are continuously making this choice in our actions, in the words that we speak, and even in the thoughts we entertain, whether we are conscious of it or not. Everything we do releases energy and creates a ripple effect in our lives and in the wider world. For this reason, the seemingly inconsequential act of looking at someone can bring them, and you, blessings or the opposite.

Looking from the Left Eye

When our thoughts, words, and actions are drawn from the Divine reservoir of Chesed and creative flow, we can be a channel of blessings. When we tap into the harsh energy of Divine Gevurah, without contextualizing our intention within an overarching frame of Chesed, we can facilitate the opposite. The power to curse and bring an *Ayin haRa* upon another person comes about through connecting to the aspect of Gevurah within the moment of Divine wrath (See *Ohr haChayim*, Bamidbar, 22:6). A person begins to embody negativity by leading a life of *Kelipah*, separation, ego and obsessive self-involvement. This negativity can then be projected through the eyes, so to speak.

The right eye and left eye distinction is relevant in this discussion. 'Right eye' energy is aligned with the attribute of Chesed and giving, much like the patriarch *Avraham* / Abraham, who had an *Ayin Tov* / Good Eye (*Avos*, 5:19). 'Left eye' power is imbalanced Gevurah, the force of withdrawal, leading to a corresponding withdrawal of life-energy. Gevurah is not inherently negative, and a left-eye perspective is often necessary in life (R. Moshe Dovid Valli, *Biur Tehilim*, 54:9), however to be balanced it needs to be in service of Chesed. When Gevurah falls out of alignment with Chesed, it can become suffocating, self-obsessed and destructive. When we view the world from this perspective, we can actually do real damage to others, as well as to ourselves.

The right eye corresponds to *Ayin Tov*, a good eye. This is the eye of Chesed; it is life-sustaining, life-affirming and quintessentially effulgent. The right eye dynamic also includes a sense of satisfaction with what you have, as well as a sense of joy for what other people have. The left eye corresponds to *Ayin haRa* / a bad eye, characterized by an unsatisfied or jealous way of seeing oneself in relation to others. The reason that *Ayin haRa* is a singular term, rather than *Einayim Ra'os* in the plural, is that it is a singular eye — the left eye. It is a 'left side' way of looking, as Gevurah is situated on the 'left side' of The Tree of Life (The Chidah, *Chasdei Avos*, 2:11). It is also a 'one-sided' way of viewing others; instead of balancing one's perspective with Chesed and sensitivity to the needs of others, the viewer is exclusively viewing the world through the constricted and constricting lens of the 'left side'.

The Torah's archetype of the *Ayin haRa* is *Bilam* / Balaam. During Israel's journey through the desert following the Exodus, the prophet Bilam was hired to curse them. What Bilam wished to do was draw down an *Ayin haRa* on the People of Israel (*Rashi*, Bamidbar, 24:2. *Tanchumah*, Balak, 6). Bilam was 'one-eyed'; he was blind in one eye (*Rashi*, Bamidbar, 24:3. *Sanhedrin*, 105a). Bilam's functional eye was the *Ayin haRa* (*Avos* 5:19. *Medrash Rabba*, Bamidbar, 20:10) — his left eye, as it were. Indeed, wherever he looked, he looked with an *Ayin haRa* (*Zohar* 1, Noach, p. 68b), and this is expressed in the deeper meaning of his name. *Bilam* is similar to the word *Bal'am* / to swallow up, draw in, or absorb (this is related to the name of the first of the eight kings of Edom or *Tohu*: Belah ben B'or; *Siach Yitzchak*, Likutim 5). Bilam looked at the world with unbalanced Gevurah, resulting in a desire to 'swallow' and withdraw life-energy, to curse, absorb and take away vitality and resources from others. This is the polar opposite of the way a Tzadik views the world through the right eye of Chesed, rooted in a desire to bless, inspire and empower others.

Throughout the episode with Bilam as recounted in the Torah, he is continuously trying to look at the People of Israel from one angle or another in order to curse them. When he first goes to curse the people it says, "And in the morning Balak (the king who hired him) took Bilam and led him up to a precipice...and from there he saw part of the people" (*Bamidbar*, 22:41). When instead of cursing, he blesses them, Balak suggests that he go to another vantage point. Balak says, "Come with me to another place from where you will see them…and curse them for me from there" (*Ibid*, 23:13). When Bilam blesses them again, Balak says: "Come now, I will take you to a different place…and you will curse them for me from there" (*Ibid*, 23:27). These three vantage points represent looking at the People of Israel via their past, present, and future. Bilam is trying to look at his subjects in any way which will cause the Ayin haRa to harm them, but he can't find a flaw which will allow the Ayin haRa to take hold. When Bilam fails to curse them a third time, Balak gives up.*

When one looks at another with an *Ayin haRa*, with envy or spite, his 'eye' unleashes negative emissions and casts *Dinim* / harsh judgments in his direction. For this reason our Sages say, "It is better for an evil person to be blind, for his eyes bring evil to the world (*Medrash Rabba*, Bamidbar, 20:2). However, it is most important to state unequivocally that those evil effects can only take hold if the other person receives and absorbs the energy. (Sadly, most people do. "99 percent of people die due to an Ayin haRa" *Baba Metziya*, 107b.) If a person is open or vulnerable to this particular form of negativity, they may receive it and integrate it into their own system and psyche. If they are not receptive or vulnerable to it, the negativity will simply bounce off them and be neutralized.

The more one believes in the negative energy being cast at them — i.e., the more one believes both in the power of the Ayin haRa to affect them, as well as in the actual judgment of their character

* Bilam wished to draw down an Ayin haRa upon Klal Yisrael, but was not able to. Therefore, to ward off an Ayin haRa, there are sources that suggest that one recite the verse: "Bilam raised his eyes (to project an Ayin haRa) and saw Israel dwelling according to its tribes, and the spirit of G-d rested upon him" (*Bamidbar*, 24:2; *Agrah DePerkah*, 72).

— the more it may have an effect upon them. Our Sages say, with regards to a similar phenomenon, "When one is particular (cares about such issues), they (the negative forces) are particular about him, however, when one is not particular, they are not particular about him" (*Pesachim*, 110b). The more a person believes in or is connected to the particular form of negativity being projected toward them, the more they open themselves up to it, and the more it can penetrate and be absorbed by their psyche. This can go on until the negativity cripples the person completely, *Chas veShalom* / Heaven forbid.

Protection from an 'Evil Eye'

Our Sages teach that a person should protect himself from an Ayin haRa (*Baba Basra*, 118a). We just mentioned that believing in negativity is a factor in being vulnerable to negative energy and its potential harm. But what if, despite our best intentions, we find that we *do* harbor at least subconscious beliefs in the power of others' judgments, jealousies, and negative projections? How might we deflect the apparently negative energy that is hurled toward us?

Our Sages advise: "If a man going into a town is afraid of the evil eye, let him take the thumb of his right hand in his left hand and the thumb of his left hand in his right hand, and say: 'I, so-and-so, am of the seed of *Yoseph* / Joseph, over which the Ayin haRa has no power'" (*Berachos*, 55b). What exactly does this mean and how does this work?

When the person takes "the thumb of his right hand in his left hand and the thumb of his left hand in his right hand," this essentially creates a closed circuit. When you do this, the intimate space of your body becomes encircled and protected from external forces. With a kind of force-field or barrier, you have created a private, insular space into which outside influences are banned entry. Nothing negative is allowed to penetrate. Inwardly, this communicates that: *I don't believe in the power of the Ayin haRa, and I don't believe in the negativity that the person looking at me is trying to project onto me.* This is the first step.

Next, you verbally affirm that you are from the seed of Yoseph, which we all are, regardless of our genealogy (See *Tehilim* 80:2). You are a protected person, like Yoseph, over whom the Ayin haRa has no sway. There were Sages who used to place themselves in situations that would normally attract envy, jealousy and an Ayin haRa. They were able to do so and remain unharmed because they were from the seed of Yoseph, and therefore believed that the Ayin haRa had no power over them (*Berachos* 20a, *Baba Metziya*, 84a. *Sotah*, 36b). This is similar to the idea that the *Mazalos* / Astrological Signs have no influence over Israel. In both cases we maintain a complete faith in Hashem, as well as in our own free-will and capacity to transform and overcome external obstacles and limitations.

Yoseph lived his own life, unlike so many whose lives are a haphazard collection of other people's impressions and expectations of what their life should look like. He was, in other words, utterly immune to his surroundings and their influences. It did not matter whatsoever if he was a slave or prisoner in Egypt, or the de facto ruler of Egypt, he was equally the Tzadik in all situations — the elevated, integrated, and spiritually committed person that he was in his father's home. Yoseph was absolutely self-confident; he believed from a very young age in his destiny of greatness. He was not swayed by other people's opinions or perceptions of him, even those of his brothers. He thus naively told his brothers that he would rule over them, and then seemed surprised that they disliked him. However, no jealousy or Ayin haRa could perturb him or sway him from his destined course.

In fact, Yoseph had the opposite effect — his vision affected the world around him, rather than the other way around.* Living in Egypt, the Egyptian women desired to gaze at him, as Yoseph was known to be very attractive. They would even climb the walls to get a glimpse of him (*Rashi*, Bereishis, 49:22), but Yoseph would not be distracted by them, nor would he set his eyes upon them (*Medrash Rabbah*, Bereishis, 97:4).

When we encircle ourselves and declare that we are like Yoseph, we affirm that we do not believe that any external Ayin haRa can harm us. As we said earlier, an ayin haRa can only have an effect on a person who believes in it. If you believe that you can be 'cursed', or that you are undeserving or unloved and therefore should be cursed, you open yourself to other people's negative energy and projections.

---

*Yoseph's power of positive sight is further illustrated by the fact that (*Zevachim*, 118b) anyone who was able to 'see' the Mishkan Shilo (the Tabernacle before the Temple was built in Yerushalayim), which was within the domain of the tribe of Yoseph, was able to eat certain types of *Kadshim* / holy foods; unlike in the Temple's time when these foods were only able to be eaten within the walls of Yerushalayim (*Zevachim*, 114). This was possible because Yoseph's holy vision had the power to sanctify all that could be seen (*Sefas Emes*, Vayechi).

For instance: a person with low self-esteem and a lack of confidence in who they are, or in the gifts that Hashem has given them, will be susceptible to an Ayin haRa and its harmful effects. People are continuously projecting energy, whether positive or negative, but only if we open ourselves up to their energy, can it have an effect on us.*

However, if a person does indeed feel a lack of spiritual, mental, emotional or physical confidence, and another person happens to look at them with jealousy or negative judgment, they may in fact imbibe these sentiments and start thinking the same corrosive thoughts about themselves. If one thinks they are bad, negative or soiled, then they will attract people, ideas and experiences which

---

* The Rambam seems to dismiss the concept of *Ayin haRa*, i.e. that a person 'looking' at another person can have a negative effect on him. Because of this, the Rambam offers alternative reasons for certain Torah laws. Here are two such examples: 1) Regarding the harm of *Hezek Re'iya* / damages caused by seeing (*Baba Basra*, 2a-b) he writes that the damage occurs in the taking away of a person's privacy, and therefore there is no Hezek Re'iya in a place where people do not live (*Hilchos Shecheinim*, 3:6). 2) Later, he writes about the law regarding a person who finds a garment and airs it out periodically, but should not do so when there are guests around. While some sources say this is because of potential Ayin haRa (*Baba Metziya*, 29b), the Rambam offers another reason (*Ibid*): because of possible theft (See *Hilchos Gezeila v'Aveida* 13:11. For a counterpoint see *Bach, Choshen Mishpat*, 267:18). While the Rambam apparently denied the *halachic* effect of the observer on the observed, it is possible that he would agree regarding the psychological effects manifest in a person who is open to the influences of the opinions and impressions of others. As we know, our psychological state has a deep effect on our physiological well-being; in other words: mental distress can impact physical health.

confirm those thoughts. As Rashi says, "Curses cleave to the cursed and blessings cannot attach themselves to a curse" (*Bereishis*, 24:39).

If you truly believe that you are good in your core, you will attract blessings into your life. If you go about knocking yourself down, you may end up being knocked down. We all need to be more like Yoseph, confident in our mission and comfortable in our own lives. Whenever you feel a bit vulnerable, make a 'circle' and say: *I am indeed from the seed of Yoseph.*

In Halacha there is a principle: a word cancels out a thought, and an action cancels out a word. If, for example, you sense that negative, jealous thoughts are directed at you, you can neutralize their effects with affirmative words such as we have mentioned: 'I am from the seed of Yoseph!' Or, 'I truly deserve what Hashem has given me!' The positive vibrations of your words will deflect the negative vibrations of that Ayin haRa. Similarly, if negative words were directed towards you, you can counter those words with positive actions. For example, if someone said that you are a selfish person, nullify these words with a positive, selfless deed.

The energy field of thoughts, words and actions that surround us is called our *Ohr Makif* / Surrounding Light. This Ohr Makif, like an aura, is a subtle external manifestation of our inner subjective state. Positive thoughts, words, and actions create a positively charged Ohr Makif that can repel any form of negativity trying to penetrate our consciousness.

The more a person believes that they are blessed, the more blessings they are open to receive and the less they need to deal with the Ayin haRa. What we really need to do is cultivate a firm and flexible belief in the inherent goodness of ourselves and our souls, as well as in the goodness of others and the world. We need to learn to see the world the way the Creator sees it: "And G-d saw..., and it was good." Relating to the world in such a way attracts even more goodness into our lives.

Developing an *Ayin Tov*

Tamuz, translated numerically, equals 453, the same value as the word *Ginas* / garden. For this reason teachers or parents are encouraged to take their young students or children out to the neighborhood gardens (R. Chayim Palagi, *Moed L'chol Chai*, 9:8, in the name of the *Targum Yonason Ben Uziel* on Megilas Esther). Perhaps, in addition to this being in response to the seasonally warm weather, this may have also been intended as an experiential means of teaching the young how to see and appreciate the world. Gardens are places of cultivated natural beauty; they are thus ideal places to identify with the potential beauty waiting to be revealed in the world. This is an active, pedagogic method to counter the Ayin haRa: consciously seeking out the beautiful, balanced and good within Hashem's creation.

The secret of developing an *Ayin Tov* / a good eye in order to see the good in others, is to begin by seeing the good in ourselves. One may start by simply finding a single point of goodness that is present within themselves. Illuminate, amplify and hold on to this good point; do not let anyone take it away from you. From that one point, it will become more possible and likely to find another point of goodness within oneself, and then another, and so on.

Our Sages tell us (*Medrash Rabbah*, Bereishis, 6:6) that on the first day of the 'season of Tamuz' nothing has a shadow. Inwardly this means that in the month of 'seeing', we are given the gift to see our true selves shining without distortion. With the Light of Creation, we are able to get a glimpse of our souls without 'shadows' or obscuration. This rectified seeing of self is the foundation of developing an Ayin Tov toward the rest of creation.

In fact, loving your neighbor begins with loving yourself — not being 'in love' with yourself, but rather, being loving toward yourself: empathizing, supporting, caring for and befriending yourself. When we see ourselves more openly, with greater kindness and less harshness or bias, then we can begin to make a Tikkun on the Ayin haRa that characterizes this month. Our positive vision will help ameliorate any outstanding harsh judgments and impact the wider world for the good.

It goes without saying that our confidence should not devolve into arrogance. We do not need to speak or act in a way that could arouse the Ayin haRa of others — even if we think we are above believing in its power. We should always try to adjust to our surroundings. This doesn't mean to be a conformist, but to be 'modest' and sensitive to those around us. When Yoseph was younger, he was so confident that he was oblivious to his brothers' feelings. As a result, his brothers turned against him and sold him into slavery.*

True confidence is balanced with humility. Self-confidence comes from the awareness that we are special and have something distinct to contribute. Humility comes from the awareness that others do as well. Arrogant or immodest self-confidence is not confidence at all, but an attempt to cover up a complete lack of confidence or a feeling of jealousy. When we are humbly confident, accepting and embracing our greatness, goodness and genius, we will merit to have an *Ayin Tov* and see the greatness, goodness and genius of others as well.

As mentioned, Avraham had an *Ayin Tov* / a good eye (*Avos*, 5:19). Because he had an Ayin Tov he also had the power to bless. Hashem tells Avraham, "and you shall be a blessing" (*Bereishis*, 12:2), which means "The blessings are entrusted into your hand" (*Medrash Rabbah, Rashi*, ibid).

To bless someone means to see a good quality hidden within them, and to empower them to draw this quality out into the open.

---

* Indeed, the entire idea of the Children of Israel being exiled in Egypt for 400 years is connected to Ayin haRa. Ayin haRa numerically equals 400 (Ayin is 130, Rah is 270 =400), thus the concept of Ayin haRa is always present when that number is mentioned. (For example: *Berachos*, 4b. *Eiruvin* 54b, *Ben Yehoyada*, ad loc.) The root of the descent into Egypt was the sale of Yoseph, toward whom the brothers projected an Ayin haRa, and were thus condemned to 400 years of exile (*Rabbeinu Bachya*, 15:13). Additionally, the 400 men of Eisav, (*Bereishis*, 32:7), and the amount of 400 *Kesef* / money paid by Avraham to acquire the Cave of Machpelah, are also both connected to Ayin haRa, (See *Rashi*, Bereishis, 34:17).

Simply acknowledging and articulating such a point of goodness that you find within another is a great blessing and help for them to more fully reveal their latent potential. But in order for a blessing to take hold, the person doing the blessing needs to find a true quality within the person. You cannot (and certainly should not) bless an untalented musician to be the next Mozart; doing so would be more of a curse than a blessing, as it is something unattainable. You therefore need to have an Ayin Tov in order to find something truly present within them, which perhaps they don't even know is there, and empower them to draw it out in a revealed manner. Indeed, much like an Ayin haRa and the curse that comes with it, the Ayin Tov, and the blessing that comes with it, needs a willing recipient. The person being blessed needs to believe in the blessing. The blessing needs to therefore focus on something that is truly present and attainable, so that they can intuitively believe in its actualization.

Ultimate Impact:

One more point needs to be mentioned with regards to the person projecting an Ayin haRa. The jealous person is himself the principal recipient of the negative impact. Projecting negativity upon others indicates that there is toxic negativity residing within one's own mind and nervous system. The way we see the world is the way we experience the world. If we are habitually discontent with our lot and life, and always jealous of other people, the biggest harm we are doing is ultimately to ourselves.

Experientially, the difference between having an Ayin haRa and having an Ayin Tov is the difference between living in 'Heaven' or living in 'hell'. Heaven is characterized by free-flowing positivity and *Chesed*, empowering and furthering life and connection. Hell is characterized by paralyzing constriction and negative *Gevurah*, fearfully diminishing or damming the flow of aliveness. In a Heaven paradigm, it's me *and* you; in hell, it's me *or* you. To live in Heaven now, we must live in a natural condition of openness, connectivity and *Fargining* (a Yiddish term for 'being happy for another person's success'). A living hell is where every person we meet is suspected of potentially taking something from us; 'if he has more, I have less'. Every interaction from this perspective brings out jealousy and enmity. The choice between Heaven and hell is ours, at any given moment. It is ultimately up to us whether we will be a blessing or a curse in the world and in the lives of others.

SIGN

EACH MONTH CONTAINS THE ZODIAC INFLUENCE OF A particular constellation, called the *Mazal*. A constellation is comprised of a perceivably patterned grouping of visible stars. Today, we count 88 constellations in the night sky. Out of all of these, one constellation is predominantly visible on the horizon at the beginning of each month.

Indeed, each constellation refracts the light of the cosmos differently, alternately reflecting times that are more conducive to war, and times that are more conducive for peace to flourish, for example (*Yalkut Reuveini, Bereishis*, Oys 56). The *Zohar* teaches that each sign can manifest positively or negatively (*Zohar* 3, 282a). In other words, the constellations can have either a productive or a destructive influence in one's life. It is important to keep in mind, however, that even if our proclivities are innate or celestially influenced, we still possess the free choice of response. In other words, we have the ability to choose how to reflect back what has been projected onto us, even from the stars. For example, a person born under the influence of Mars may have a tendency to be involved with blood, but he or she also has the ability to employ this inherent tendency for good or ill; such a person could therefore choose to be a violent criminal or a life-saving surgeon.

Due to the prevailing popular belief that the stars exert a kind of fatalistic influence upon world history and human development, we need to repeatedly emphasize that anyone can rise above these influences altogether and be unaffected by them. Despite all the forces and influences in our life — physical and psychological conditions, upbringing, education, environment, financial status, etc. — we always have the freedom to choose. We have the choice to live as either the *effect* of our conditions (as passive receivers of what life serves us), or as the *cause* of what comes next, thereby becoming proactive co-creators of our lives. When we begin to live more proactively, the influences of our birth constellation and the *Mazal* of each month function less as positive or negative *influences*, and more as *tools* that can help us climb ever higher into our freedom of being.

Sartan / the Crab, or Cancer, is the astrological sign of Tamuz. It is said that hot weather causes crabs to procreate and multiply. The nature of the crab is to hide within its thick shell and bury itself within the crevices at the seashore. Many refer to the Crab as 'the dark constellation,' as it is the least brilliant group of stars in the sky. It is almost as if it is hiding from the harshness of the month itself.

Commenting on the Sefer Yetzirah, the Raavad writes that the *Sartan* is a creature of the sea and is thus associated with water. There are two types of water, salty and fresh, alluding to two kinds of tears. There are tears of joy, which open and clear the eyes in order to reveal hidden goodness or meaning, and there are tears of despondency, which dim or cloud the eyes, resulting in further concealment of goodness or purpose. Tears of despondency, as explored earlier, are connected to the verse that mentions the women who cried for the idol Tamuz.

Cancerians are generally emotional people and can be prone to 'hot-headed' over-reactivity. The month of Tamuz is a time of extreme physical heat, which represents this emotional heat. Cancerians are also domestic people who feel a strong bond to their families and homes. They have a strong value for history and relationship to the past, which can be constructive or constrictive. Another trait among Cancerians is to move like a crab — sideways, in a manner of avoidance. That is, they are prone to expressing their emotions and needs indirectly rather than openly in order to avoid conflict.

Directly addressing our suffering, and directly embracing our deeper spiritual needs, creates a Tikkun for the month of Tamuz. Properly mourning spiritual, historical, familial and natural destruction in this month will eventually lead us from despondency to clarity and joy. Tears of suffering may temporarily blur our vision, but with a good cry, the tears of bitterness will be transformed into tears of hope. When the initial emotion passes, after a good cry, our eyes sparkle and we are able to see with greater clarity than ever before. This is a profound metaphor (*Bnei Yissaschar*, Tamuz, Maamar 4:5). In times of hardship, it can be hard to see anything at all, including yourself, other people or the reality of your situation. Yet, after a cleansing cry, your vision of life can become more crystallized than ever. Your life, your past, even your sufferings can take on a whole new meaning when seen through the tear-filled eyes of Redemption.

The months of Tamuz and Av are symbolized by two weeping eyes, in the words of the Prophet: "My eyes, my eyes, pour water..." (*Eicha*, 1:16). Tamuz and Av also contain major fast days, and refraining from eating causes a 'darkening' of the eyes, as it says: "My eyes are lit up, because I have tasted [eaten]" (*Shmuel* I, 14:29). The spiritual practices of Tamuz and Av gently guide us through a heartbreaking labyrinth of history into a deep recognition and healing embrace of all the darkness, bitterness and brokenness in ourselves and in the world. From within the ruins of our inner and outer 'Temples', tears well up and obscure our vision, but only momentarily. As the bitter waters begin to flow, they are gradually transformed into the fresh, sweet waters of Redemption. This is the transformative potential of Tamuz. It is specifically by going deeper into our darkness that we are able to reveal the highest light.

♈

TRIBE

*E*VERY MONTH OF THE YEAR IS CONNECTED WITH ONE OF the Twelve Tribes of Israel, the sons of *Yaakov* / Jacob (*Sefer Yetzirah*; Medrash, *Osyos Rebbe Akiva*, Dalet).

Reuven / Reuben, the eldest son of the twelve tribes, is the tribe associated with the month of Tamuz. His name means *Re'u* / see, *Ben* / my child. When he was born, his mother Leah said, "Hashem has *seen my suffering* and now my husband will love me" (*Bereishis*, 29:32). Leah suffered for many years prior to this, as she felt unloved by Yaakov, and her eyes were dim and tender from all the bitter tears she had shed (*Ibid*, 29:17). However, when Hashem 'sees' her, a child is born and she gains clarity and joy.

Yaakov loves Rachel, but is tricked into marrying Leah. He is not able to see the face of his bride beneath her veil on their wedding night until after they unite and conceive Reuven. In a way, this story is about a reversal of what is 'seen'; things are not always as they appear, for often reality is 'concealed.' Yaakov 'sees' or feels he should marry only his beloved Rachel, yet Hashem sees that it would be best for him to first marry Leah and to bear children with her. He has to be with Leah, whose eyes are dimmed by tears of suffering, before he can be with Rachel, the one who is 'beautiful to see.' In the end, however, it is Leah who lives a full life with Yaakov, and it is she who is buried next to him.

Reuven corresponds to the idea of vision in general, but more specifically to higher vision: the ability to see past the surface of things as they appear. The name Reuben can also be read as *Re'u* / see, *Bein* / between. This is the power of 'seeing in between the lines', beyond what is normally perceived. We should, indeed, look directly and honestly at the suffering and negativity of the world, and even shed tears, but we should also see past surface appearances to the changeless goodness underlying everything. This is the work of Tamuz — to see and discern "in between" all the suffering and hardships the potential and presence of light and purpose. Seeing concealed goodness is a fundamental aspect of the Tikkun of our eyes, which we are aspiring to achieve in this month of sight and suffering.

Often, it is precisely through the perception of darkness and experience of hardships that our vision becomes crystallized and we are able to see more clearly. Many times, it is through the valley of tears that our doors of perception are cleansed and we can, for the first time, truly see. The book of *Yechezkel* / Ezekiel is a book of prophecy composed in exile, outside the Land of Israel, after the destruction of the first Holy Temple. A people downtrodden and beaten are put in chains and forced to march to Babylon, and there in the midst of exile, a great prophet arises from the ashes. It was on "the fifth day of the fourth month (Tamuz) I (Yechezkel) saw a vision of Hashem…I looked, and behold, a large cloud, a blistering fire" (*Yechezkel*, 1). The Master Prophet goes on to describe one of the greatest mystical visions ever encountered. Here he is, during the month of Tamuz, sitting on the banks of a river in Babylon, with a people dispersed and in distress, and this is precisely when and where he experiences one of the most profound visions of Divinity ever recorded. This is because "our (deeper) vision comes not from the white of the eye, but rather from the black (pupil)" (*Medrash Rabbah*, Vayikra 31:8). It was through the hardship and tears of exile that his vision was cleansed and sharpened so that he was able to behold the Divine Chariot.

Appropriately, the *Yam haMelach* / Dead Sea, or 'sea of salt,' neighbors the portion of land apportioned to the tribe of Reuven when the People of Israel settled the land. This is highly symbolic, as Reuven is connected to a higher, deeper form of seeing which comes through hardship and (salty water) tears.

☾

BODY PART

ꭼ ACH MONTH IS CONNECTED WITH THE GENERAL ENERGY and particular vibration of a specific body part. This interinclusion of body within time empowers one to focus on and refine the spiritual properties and miraculous functionings of their physical body, as the spiral of the yearly cycle continues to turn on its Divine axis.

The body part associated with Tamuz is the right hand. The right side is an allusion to Chesed. An outstretched hand, with the index finger extended is a universal sign of 'pointing,' signaling for others to look in a certain direction. ("The right hand writes and *points...*" *Medrash Tehilim* (also known as *Medrash Shochar Tov*) Chap 35:2). This is a clear connection between the body part and the sense of the month, seeing.

'Pointing' alludes to Redemption: "Each Tzadik will point with his finger and say, 'This is our G-d for whom we have waited, that He might save us. This is Hashem for whom we have hoped, we will be glad and rejoice in His salvation. (*Ta'anis*, 31a, quoting *Yeshayahu*, 25:9)'"

As hinted with regard to the sense of sight, by means of the tears and hardships of exile our eyes become clarified. They thus become holy instruments capable of envisioning and beholding a new reality and a redeemed world. They only need to be 'pointed' in the right direction. In the words of the Prophet Yeshayahu, in relation to the Final Redemption: "*Se'u Saviv Einayich*.../ Lift up your eyes and look around, they all gather together, they come to you. Your sons will come from afar, and your daughters will be carried in their arms. Then you will see and be radiant, and your heart will thrill and rejoice (*Yeshayahu*, 60:4-5)." It is precisely through the hardship and weeping of exile that we receive and perceive the clear vision of Redemption. Finally, we are able to "lift up our eyes" and see the shimmering reality of Chesed that the prophets and Tzadikim have been pointing out to us all along.

Our vision of the future is often predicated on how we have seen things in the past. Experientially, when we are going through hardship, or G-d forbid a tragedy, one of the things that pulls us through is that in the past we *have* known joy, love and blessings. Because we have already known some measure of goodness, we can reclaim goodness for our future. This deeper knowledge is itself like a 'pointing finger', a hand of Chesed guiding our focus away from despondency and toward the underlying goodness of life.

If something was built and then destroyed, we know that it can be rebuilt again. This is true in the life of an individual, on a microcosmic level, and also true on a macrocosmic level. We know that one day, starting right now, the world will be redeemed, creation will be perfected, there will be peace, harmony, brother- and sisterhood and "the occupation of the entire world will be solely to know Hashem" (Rambam, *Hilchos Melachim*, 12:5). We know that one day we will be able to see Hashem's presence and that "the glory of Hashem will be revealed, and all people will *see* it together" (*Yeshayahu*, 40:5). We know the future because we know the past. There was once a time when we were liberated from our exile in Egypt and guided by Hashem's Hand through the Desert. We will thus most certainly be redeemed again.

The 'two weeping eyes' of the present exile have their counterpoint in the two clear eyes of Hashem's revelation to us in the past: "For you have revealed to them *Ayin b'Ayin* / eye-to-eye, face-to-face" (*Bamidbar*, 14:14). To encounter a person or the Creator "eye-to-eye" is to see deeply, with total clarity of vision. This alludes specifically to the Revelation of the Torah at Mount Sinai, where we could *see the sounds* of the Divine Word tangibly.

According to the Ramban, the whole purpose of the *Mishkan* / Tabernacle and the *Mikdash* / Holy Temple is to recreate the Revelation of Sinai, to make that revelatory experience perpetually palpable for all people (Ramban, *Shemos* 25:2). With regards to the Mikdash, it says: "Just as you come to see with two eyes, you have come to be seen by two eyes" (*Chagigah*, 2a). This means that when you go to the Temple, you can 'see' Hashem's presence as with your own two eyes; but also, Hashem can see you, as it were, with two eyes. This is a face-to-face, eye-to-eye encounter with the Divine Presence.

As the beginning of the destruction of both Temples occurred in this month, "My eyes, my eyes, pour water/tears" (*Eicha*, 1:16). In the end, however, we will merit seeing eye-to-eye with Hashem: "For eye to eye they shall see, when Hashem returns to Zion" (*Yeshayahu*, 52:8).

♈

ELEMENT

*T*HERE ARE FOUR PRIMARY ELEMENTS, FOUR FUNDAMENTAL building blocks of creation: fire, air, water and earth. Each month is associated with one of these four elements. However, it is important to note that while manifesting physically, these elements are also meant to be understood in a much more metaphysical sense as well, as they represent numerous properties, qualities, and correspondences.*

Tamuz is related to the element of water. Water is related not

---

* For a more in-depth exploration of these elements and their relationship to the Hebrew calendar, please see the introductory volume of this series: *The Spiral of*

only to tears, as previously discussed, but also to desire (*Sha'ar haKe-dusha*, Sha'ar 1) and intense emotions of other kinds, "as the sound of many waters…" (*Tehilim*, 93). In the physically hot month of Tamuz, one may experience the 'heat' of emotional over-sensitivity and re-activity. Water is a universal antidote to heat, having the ability to bring coolness and refreshment, as well as the ability to extinguish fire. Water also brings purification, such as when one immerses in the waters of a *Mikvah* / a transformational pool of living wa-ters. Holy tears, too, purify our eyes and minds. Water clarifies and distinguishes between holy love and despondent love-sickness, as in "Many waters cannot extinguish (true) love" (*Shir haShirim*, 8:7). When we connect to these qualities embodied in water, we can extinguish the fires of negative yearnings and desires, cleanse our hearts and reveal true love.

☽

Time: Unraveling the Yearly Cycle.

ת

TORAH PORTIONS

O VER THE COURSE OF A MONTH, 4-5 WEEKLY TORAH
portions are read by the community. These individual portions can be combined and viewed as a single
unit based on the particular month in which they are most commonly read. Indeed, one finds, when viewing the *Parshas* through
this calendrical lens, that an astounding array of thematic elements
consistent with the spiritual energy of the month are revealed.

Appropriately, we find that sight and jealousy are the two main
themes of this month's Torah portions, namely Shelach, Korach,
Chukas and Balak. In Parshas Shelach, Moshe sends the *Meraglim*
/ spies or scouts to "see the Land" (*Bamidbar* 13:18). They report 'seeing' a place which they did not desire (*Ibid*, 32:33). Most of the actual
'seeing' of the Land took place during the month of Tamuz. Moshe

wanted them to have a positive spiritual vision of the Land of Israel, and to thereby affect the Land positively (*Baba Basra*, 56a). They were actually meant to 'acquire' the Land by looking at it. They did the reverse, however, and by focusing on the negative, they prolonged their acquisition of the Land, and made the process that much more difficult for themselves.

The Meraglim did not see the Land the way it really was, but rather the way *they* were — scared and insecure in their mission. They thus projected a negative vision of themselves onto the Land: "And there we saw the giants in the Land…we appeared in our own eyes as grasshoppers — and so were we in their eyes" (*Bamidbar*, 13:33).

The Meraglim, who were in fact the leaders of each of the twelve respective tribes, had no way of knowing how they were perceived in the eyes of the inhabitants of the Land. In their own view, however, they were unfit and inferior, and so they assumed that their perception was accurate. The outcome was that they did not have the will to enter the Land. They also figured that if they went into the Land, they would no longer remain as the heads of their tribes, and the prospect of having new leadership caused them to become jealous. The end of Parshas Shelach speaks of 'seeing' the *Tzitzit* (*Ibid*, 14:39). The Mitzvah of Tzitzit is specifically referred to as a Tikkun for the eyes; the very act of seeing them is meant to remind one of the entire Torah and essence of what it means to be a Jew in the world.

In Parshas Korach, Korach is 'jealous' of Moshe and Aharon. His vision of reality is skewed, as he focuses only on the negative within others. Rashi asks: "What did Korach '*see*' to decide to quarrel with Moshe?" (*ibid*, Rashi, 16:7); i.e., how was Korach's vision distorted to the extent that he made such a monumental error in judgment? In the morning after his challenges to Moshe, however, it becomes clear for all to see who should be the Kohen Gadol. Korach's rebellion only brings increased stature to Aharon, the rightful Kohen, in the eyes of the people.

Parshas Chukas begins with the laws of the *Parah Adumah* / the Red Heifer, a ritual designed to bring purity and clarity to those who have been in contact with death. Chukas also mentions the copper snake, a visual image which healed those who were bitten by vipers (*ibid*, 21:8). The bronze snake was held high so that as people raised their eyes to gaze at the snake, they were really looking upward toward the 'Heavens' (*Rosh Hashanah*, 3:8). This redirection of their vision helped them turn their lives around toward the Source of Life and thereby gain healing and protection from negativity.

Parshas Balak is about negative vision (*Ibid*, 22:1). Balak, the jealous king, envisions cursing the People of Israel. Bilam, the dark prophet, is 'blind in one eye,' meaning he has an Ayin haRa and intentionally looks for negativity in order to amplify and exploit it for his benefit (*Avos*, 5:19). According to the Zohar, wherever his eye would look it would cause destruction (*Zohar* 1, 68b). However, in the end, despite his intentions, Bilam sees only the positive in the People of Israel camped in the desert before him, and gives them the loftiest of blessings (*Bamidbar*, 24:2).

In the story of Pinchas, Pinchas sees great negativity occurring in the community, including licentious behavior and idol-worship

(*Ibid*, 25:7), but he also maintains a higher vision of who the People of Israel can be. He therefore takes radical, even violent, action in order to 'break the spell' and stop the plague from spreading through the camp. Because of his radical response, he is indeed able to stop the plague. However, following his complicated but heroic action, he is then blessed with a *Bris Shalom* / a Covenant of Peace. One wonders whether this blessing was in some way a Tikkun for Pinchas's violent response to the situation. Especially during the month of Tamuz, when we are focused so intently on not letting the 'heat' of the season overwhelm or push us in destructive directions, we can more clearly see the complexity of Pinchas's story. His reception of the Covenant of Peace following such an episode provides a subtle commentary to his particular handling of the situation, no matter how efficacious it was in the moment. The blessing of the Bris Shalom is in effect the last word in the story, contextualizing Pinchas's valorization within a broader Torah worldview.

༯

SEASON OF THE YEAR

*T*HE SEASONAL QUALITIES OF EACH MONTH ARE INTRICATELY related with the spiritual energies of that month. When daylight lasts for either longer or shorter times, different kinds of spiritual light are being revealed on a subtle level. The physical experiences of spring are external expressions of an internal reality emanating during that time, such as the vital pulse of new life and growth. All dark and dank months reflect an energy of corresponding spiritual 'coldness', stimulating us to seek warmth. People tend to keep to themselves when winter begins and are more outgoing when summer starts. All of these psycho-physical weather patterns reflect deeper spiritual truths, as the mind-body complex is a reflection of the metaphysical qualities of the soul and spiritual realm.

The longest days of the year are in the month of Tamuz, which is generally also the hottest month of the year. Spiritually, Tamuz is the harshest month of the year, even more so than the following month of Av. As will be explored in more depth throughout the second half of this book, Av is harsh only through the first fourteen days, but in the second half of Av, the temperature decreases and the energy lightens up. As the intensity of the sun diminishes, so does the intensity of the spiritual harshness. The month of Tamuz, however, is intense and harsh throughout, and therefore we need to be mindful and take precautions. We also need to embrace, and productively integrate, the sense of real hardship that may manifest during this time.

The discomfort of extreme physical heat naturally leads to emotional heat and inner irritation. Emotions and tempers can run high during this month, leading people to act out in wild, unbecoming ways. In popular culture, immodest exposure is at its peak, which creates an idolatrous worship of the body, along with harmful jealousy and an exile of true human dignity. From a more elevated perspective, however, the intense emotions of this time may be raised and channeled towards passionately revealing the Divine presence within the world and 'exposing' the true goodness of who we are.

This time of year can also stimulate a sense of loss and grief, giving us an opportunity to elevate sadness. While it is always good and perhaps even a Mitzvah to be happy, we also need to learn to allow ourselves to feel the intensity of human sadness. To do this, we can gather all the sadness and brokenness that arose during the past year, which we may have pushed aside when it originally arose, and allow ourselves to feel its full intensity. Allow yourself to grieve for any losses, any devolution of your physical or spiritual condition, any unrealized goals, damaged relationships or misfortunes. Open yourself sympathetically to those in your world who are in deep need of health, happiness, clarity, livelihood or a good *Shidduch* / match. Meditate on the cosmic pain of the exile of the *Shechinah* / the Presence of the Divine in this world. Allow yourself to have a good, cleansing cry. Turn your tears into prayers.

According to some sources, the first day of Tamuz is when Moshe struck the rock (*Machzor Vitri*, 14). As a result of this mistake, he died in the Desert and never reached the Promised Land of Israel. This personal 'exile' for Moshe became, in a sense, the exile of the entire nation. In Tamuz, we mark the beginning of our present exile, when the walls of Jerusalem were breached (the first Temple on the 9th of Tamuz, and the second Temple on the 17th of Tamuz, *Ta'anis*, 28b. *Tur*, Orach Chayim, p. 549. Although see Yerushalmi, *Ta'anis*, 4:5 and *Tosefos*, Rosh Hashanah, 18b), which eventually led to the destruction of the Beis haMikdash and our traumatic expulsion from the Land.

As mentioned, Tamuz is when the *Meraglim* / scouts that Moshe sent were viewing the Land. The Torah says that this time period was *Y'mei Bikurei Anavim* / the season of the first ripe grapes (*Bamidbar* 13:20). Reb Shimshon Ostropoli, the great Seventeenth Century Tzadik, teaches that the letters that precede each of the individual letters of the word *Anavim* are Samach-Mem-Aleph-Lamed, spelling *Sam-E-l* / Divine Poison, or the Satanic force (See *Bnei Yissaschar*, Tamuz-Av, Ma'amar 2:11). This idea is also reflected in our Sages' teaching that the *Ketev Meriri*, a group of *Sheidim* / demons, have particularly strong influence during this month (*Pesachim*, 111b), especially between the time period from the 17th of Tamuz until the 9th of Av (*Medrash Rabbah*, Eicha 3:29. The Torah mentions Ketev Meriri, *Devarim*, 29:24. *Rashi* (ad loc) writes that their name is merely Meriri).

However the above teaching is understood (i.e., whether Sheidim are expressions of metaphysical objective energy, 'demons within' [i.e.; psychological seasonal disorder], or a hybrid of both), the point is that during this month and the first ten or so days of Av, there is an increase of negative forces in the universe; it is thus a time to be on guard against lurking spiritual dangers and bubbling intense emotions. While opening ourselves up to experience the harshness and brokenness within our lives, we need to ensure that our tears do not lead to depression, but rather to greater clarity and ultimate hope.

THE HOLIDAY OF THE MONTH:
The 17th of Tamuz

IN THE MONTHS THAT CONTAIN A YOM TOV / HOLIDAY, THAT *Yom Tov* embodies and encapsulates the energy of the entire month in condensed form. In a month that does not have a major holiday, that absence is also an expression of the unique energy of the month.

"For everything there is an appointed time" (*Koheles*, 3:1). In other words, everything happens according to Divine timing (Rebbe RaYatz, *Sefer haMa'amorim*, tof/shin/aleph, p. 59). Our Sages tell us that when we left Egypt, it was the appointed time for such liberation. This means not only that it occurred in the historically appropriate time, but also at the right time of year — the season best suited for this expression of Redemption. This is the same principle behind every *Yom Tov*.

Shiva-Asar b'Tamuz / the 17th of Tamuz is a day of fasting that initiates the "Three Weeks of Mourning" until the 9th of Av. This time period is called *Bein haMetzarim* / between the narrow straits, and contains various laws and practices such as refraining from eating meat, drinking wine and other activities (*Shulchan Aruch*, Orach Chayim, Mechaber and Remah, 551:2-4- 9-15-17). This is based on a verse in *Eicha* / Lamentations: כָּל־רֹדְפֶיהָ הִשִּׂיגוּהָ בֵּין הַמְּצָרִים / All her pursuers overtook her in between the narrow straits (*Eicha*, 1:3). The time period between the 17th of Tamuz and the 9th of Av is thus called 'between the narrow straits.' Yet, as the verse clearly states, "all pursuers overtook her" which means, according to the Magid of Kaznitch, that any person who truly desires her (i.e., desires to get close to Hashem during this time) can more easily do so than at other times of the year. It is a harsh time period to be sure, a time of *Din* / judgement, yet despite this, or perhaps because of this, it is also a time we can more easily feel close to Hashem. This dynamic is further indicated by the word *Eicha* itself, which can, according to the Medrash, also be read as *Ayeka* / where are you? (*Medrash Eichah Rabba*, Pesichta, 4). When read in this way, as an existential question or spiritual call to awareness, it becomes clear that all of our sufferings are ultimately meant to wake us up to our higher self and purpose, if we but heed the call.

Historically, many tragedies took place on the 17th of Tamuz. Five of these tragedies are emphasized by our Sages:

1) Moshe smashed the *Luchos* / Tablets when he saw the people wildly worshipping the *Egel haZahav* / Golden Calf. Eventually, Moshe came down with a second set of Luchos, which represents the beginning of the revealing of *Torah Sheba'al*

Peh / the Oral Tradition, which includes the redemptive teachings of the Inner Dimensions of Torah.

2) During the Babylonian siege on Jerusalem in the First Temple Era, the Jews were forced to stop offering daily sacrifices due to a lack of cattle.

3) Apostomus, the leader of the Roman occupiers of Israel, burned the Torah.

4) An idol was placed in the Holy Temple by the Romans.

5) The walls of Jerusalem were breached by the Romans in 69 CE. Three weeks later, despite a courageous struggle on the part of the Jews, the Romans destroyed the Second Holy Temple.

According to the Jerusalem Talmud, the 17th of Tamuz is also the day the Babylonians breached the walls of Jerusalem on their way to destroying the First Temple (*Ta'anis*, 4:5. See *Yirmiyahu*, 52:4-8. *Rosh Hashanah*, 18b. *Tosefos*, Zeh Tisha). This was after Tzidekiah, the Judean king, and his soldiers all fled the holy city. Furthermore, after fleeing to *Yericho* / Jericho, the king's entire force left him stranded. This abandonment by the king's troops is another vivid metaphor for the dynamics and energy of this time period. Tamuz is a time in which we consider all the ways that we have abandoned The True King and Master of the Universe, thereby causing the metaphysical destruction of the 'Temple Above' which led to the destruction of the 'Temple Below' (*Sanhedrin*, 96b. *Nefesh HaChayim*, Sha'ar 1:4).

Despite all of these negative associations, the number 17 is numerically equal to the word *Tov* / 'good'. The word *Tov* begins with the letter Tes, which represents 'hidden goodness', as the first time the letter Tes appears in the Torah is in the word *Tov*, describing the 'Hidden Light' of Creation.* The shape of the letter Tes turns inward, hinting at the Tov haGanuz / Hidden Goodness that is enfolded within our worldly reality.

When Moshiach is finally revealed and the world is redeemed we will be able to 'see' the once-hidden Light of Creation and ultimate Goodness. According to the commentator's calculations, Boaz married Ruth and conceived a child on the 17th of Tamuz (90+ days since her conversion. *Derashas Chasam Safer*). Boaz married Ruth; on that very night she became pregnant (*Ruth*, 4:16) and Boaz passed away (*Yalkut Shimoni*, 608). The child Ruth conceived on the night of their wedding was Oved, the grandfather of King David, who, as we know, is the archetypal progenitor of Moshiach. So, it was that very night of joy followed by mourning that brought about the birth and kindled the spark of Moshiach.

Tes is numerically 9, and adding 17 creates the sum of 26, the numerical value of the Name of Hashem (Yud/10 + Hei/5 + Vav/6 + Hei/5 = 26). Thus, within the 17th of Tamuz is hidden the Name of Hashem. Hiding within the negativity of this time there is Divine compassion, light and goodness, which will be fully revealed with the coming of Moshiach. **

---

*The first time a letter appears in the beginning of a word in the Torah is directly representative of the underlying quality of that particular letter. *Toldos Yitzchok* by a Talmid of Reb Rav Isaac Chover, p. 39b. See also *Bnei Yissachar*, Iyyar, Ma'amar 3. See *Baba Kamah*, 55a.

**According to the prevailing opinion, there is nothing 'inherently' negative on the 17th of Tamuz. Yet, the Chasam Sofer suggests otherwise (See also *Magen Avraham*, Orach Chayim, 551), that (from) the 17th of Tamuz there is a negative

Strengthening this idea is the fact that the Divine name *A'ha'va'h* (which is connected to overcoming distances) is numerically 17 (Aleph/1 + Hei/5 + Vav/6 + Hei/5). Also, in the Name of Hashem, the Yud is sometimes counted as 1 instead of 10. In this way, the numerical values of the four letters are, in order: Yud/1, Hei/5, Vav/6, Hei/5, the sum of which is 17. When Redemption finally arrives, and Hashem's love is fully revealed, the 17th of Tamuz will be transformed into a Yom Tov / Celebratory Day of complete clarity and joy, rather than one of mourning and fasting as it is now (Rambam, *Hilchos Ta'anis* 5:19; *Rosh Hashanah*, 18b).

Interestingly, the Torah itself specifies the 17th of Tamuz as a holiday. On the 16th of Tamuz, when Aaron saw the Golden Calf that was about to be worshipped, he said, "*Tomorrow* shall be a festival to Hashem" (*Shemos*, 32:5. "Tomorrow" can also mean any other time in the future [*Rashi*, Devarim, 6:20], alluding to the eventual Yom Tov of the 17th of Tamuz. *Beis Aharon*, Pinchas. Chidah, *Nachal Kadmonim*, Ki Tisa, 10). Aaron's intention was simply to delay the idolatrous worship another day until Moshe would return, but the Torah does call it a festival day nonetheless. Indeed, if no Golden Calf would have been erected, there would have been no breaking of the Luchos. Moshe would have descended the mountain with the Luchos on the 17th of Tamuz, and it would have been an ecstatic celebration of the receiving of the Torah. Even though it didn't happen that way, the potential for it remains deeply imprinted within the spiritual substructure of the day, just waiting to be activated. This is the hidden dimension of *Tov*, and of Yom Tov, within the 17th of Tamuz.

'energy' in the world. *Torahs Moshe*, Shavuos, p. 598. So much so, that if Moshe would have descended with the Luchos on the 16th of Tamuz, he would have not broken them.

If not for the Golden Calf and the breaking of the Luchos, every month of the year would have a Yom Tov. The month of Nisan has Pesach, Iyyar has *Pesach Katan* / the 'Small Pesach', Sivan has Shavuos, Tamuz has a *Yom Tov Gadol* / a great Yom Tov, and so forth (*Yalkut Shimoni*, Pinchas, 782. Chidah. *Devarim Achadim*, Derush 20. See also; *Pesikta d'Rav Kehanah*, Piska 30). But because of the *Kilkul* / damage that occurred on the 17th of Tamuz, the holidays of Tamuz, Av and Elul were all moved to Tishrei. Based on this teaching, we can deduce that Rosh Hashanah would have been in Tamuz, Yom Kippur would have been in Av, Sukkos in Elul and Shemini Atzeres in Tishrei. The 17th of Tamuz would have been not only a *Yom Tov Gadol* marking the completion of the giving of the Torah (a process that began in Sivan, marked by Shavuos), but it would also have been Rosh Hashanah.

Deep within the darkness and tragedy of Tamuz and Av, there is a hidden element of light and celebration. There is *Tov* / goodness and light, and there is *Yom Tov* / Festal Celebration. Indeed, the tribe of the month, Reuven, is connected to "the Light of *Chesed* / Kindness" (Arizal, *Likutei Torah*, Vayetze), and the "Gate of Goodness" (*Heichal haBeracha*, Bamidbar, 13:4). Even as we meditate during this time on embracing the suffering and brokenness in our lives and in the whole world, we should remain aware of the fact that light is always hiding within darkness, waiting to be revealed. Ultimately, it is within the deepest darkness that the potential for the brightest light is concealed in gestation.

☾

REDEMPTION WITHIN EXILE

Yoseph, who embodies the ability to ward off all *Ayin haRa* / negative seeing, was born on the first day of Tamuz (*Yalkut Shimoni*, Shemos, 1). Yoseph was a master of exile. Even when displaced from his family and land, he flourished and became a powerful nurturer and source of *Shefa* / abundance to those around him. He found light, purpose and direction where others would have found only darkness and confusion. Having been sold by his brothers into slavery, he could honestly tell them upon reuniting, "Indeed, you intended evil against me, [but] Hashem designed it for good" (*Bereishis*, 50:20). He was thus able to see the light, purpose and bigger picture in every situation.

On the Third of Tamuz, *Yehoshua* / Joshua stopped the movement of the sun in the sky (*Yehoshua* 10:12-14. *Avodah Zarah*, 25a. The Tzadik (and General Soul) of each generation is likened to the sun; *Kidushin*, 72b. *Shir HaShirim* Rabbah 1:5. *Gimel Tamuz* / 3rd of Tamuz marks the passing of the 'sun' of our generation, the Lubavitcher Rebbe of blessed, righteous memory). The regular cycle of the sun expresses the world of Din: the rhythm of predictability, rigidity, order and the constrictions of space and time. Yehoshua was able to transcend this Din and the corresponding confinement of mechanistic natural law. It is not that he caused the sun to cease functioning altogether, rather he mastered it and employed it to reveal the victory of hidden light over revealed light.

The Three Weeks of mourning — from the 17th of Tamuz through the 9th of Av — number 21 days. This is the same number of days of Yom Tov throughout the year; Rosh Hashanah is two days (even in the Temple Era, there were often two days of Rosh Hashanah [*Rosh Hashanah* 30b]), and Yom Kippur is one day. Sukkos is seven days, and Shemini Atzeres is one day. Pesach is seven days, and Shavuos is one day. We also count one day for Shabbos and one day for Rosh Chodesh, bringing the sum to 21 — [2+1+7+1+7+1+1+1=21]. In fact, it is during these 'Three Weeks' that we read the Parsha of Pinchas, where all the holidays of the year are mentioned and described. This means that the meta-root of all the sacred days of the year are hidden within these 'dark' days of The Three Weeks.*

Furthermore, these 21 days of mourning also parallel the 21 days in the month of Tishrei between Rosh Hashanah and Hoshana Rabbah (*Maharsha*, Bechoros, 8a). The days of mourning are days of 'concealment' and the days of Tishrei are days of 'revelation' (*Maor Vashemesh*, Parshas Pinchas). These two categories are like two sides of a coin. The breaching of the walls in Tamuz culminates in the utter destruction of the Temple in Av. The Day of Judgment and responsibility (Rosh Hashanah) culminates in a festival of seven days of utter joy, Sukkos, when we erect the "fallen tent of David."

In our lives, there are 'high' times like the *Chagim* / Festivals, and there are also 'low' times like the weeks of mourning in Tamuz and Av. The truth is, the highs and lows are really expressions of the same Divine intention of redeeming and healing humanity.

---

* This 21-day period represents a transformative cycle that 'hastens' the revelation of previously concealed potential, as the verse states: "And the word of Hashem came to me, saying, "'What do you see, Yirmiyahu?' And I said, 'I see a rod of an almond tree.' And Hashem said to me, 'You have seen well, for I hasten My word to accomplish it' (*Yirmiyahu*, 1:11-12). Upon which the Medrash states (*Eichah Rabba*, Pesichta, 23): "Just as an almond takes 21 days from its inception to blos-

Even in our moments of exile, there is concealed, eternal light — the 'Hidden Light' of Redemption.

Our task includes fully embracing our darkness and sadness in such a way that our eyes are cleansed and focused. Our spiritual eyes will then open to recognize and uncover the Hidden Light (the sparks of meaning and purpose), even within the exile. When we embrace both the 'ups and the downs of life' we will see that the descents are only there to bring us to a more clarified, luminous and stable state of elevation.

The 21 days of mourning and the 21 days of Yom Tov comprise 42 days in total, which hint at the 42 journeys of the Children of Israel in the Desert from the time they left Egypt until reaching the Promised Land (*Bamidbar*, 31:1). These, in turn, symbolize the 42 spiritual journeys that we each take in our lives, gradually moving from exile, darkness, confusion and destruction into redemption, light, clarity and the building up of life and holiness.

☾

---

som, the same is true for the process that takes place between the 17th of Tamuz and the 9th of Av."

DEEPER INTENTIONS FOR 'THE THREE WEEKS'

The Arizal teaches that during The Three Weeks between the 17th of Tamuz and the 9th of Av, also called the Days of *Meitzarim* / constrictions, we should use a special *Kavanah* / intention in our Amidah prayers. When we say the words *Baruch Atah Hashem* / You are the Source of all Blessings, while pronouncing the Divine name *Ado-nai*, we should simultaneously envision the letters Tes-Dalet-Hei-Dalet. This is an 'alternative spelling' of the Divine name, composed of the letters preceding each of the letters Yud, Hei, Vav and Hei.

The first part of this meditative 'name', Tes-Daled, has a numerical value of 13. This number represents the 13 days from the 17th of Tamuz until the end of the month. During this period, there is a concealment of the Thirteen Attributes of Compassion (*Shemos*, 34:6-7). In the imminent Redemption, this period will become a revelation of the Thirteen Attributes, and thus a time of great joy and healing.

The second part of the 'name', Hei-Dalet, has a value of 9. This represents the Nine Days of mourning in the beginning of Av. These days, in turn, correspond to the nine attributes of *Zeir Anpin* / the Small Face of Compassion, which is a transcendent aspect of Divinity (*Bamidbar*, 14:18-19).

With this meditative focus, whenever we recite a blessing throughout The Three Weeks, we can make a Tikkun for our eyes and transform *Din* by envisioning and seeing the Divine Compassion present within all people and all Creation. We can thus stimulate a process of transcending, fixing and redeeming the brokenness and suffering of the world.

꒰ঌ

PRACTICE

*T*AMUZ IS A MONTH IN WHICH WE NEED TO REFINE OUR vision and our eyes. This includes more consciously choosing both *what* and *how* we look at the world and ourselves.

The first and vital step is *Shemiras Einayim* / protection of the eyes. What we see has a profound effect on our psyche. The things we perceive, whether consciously or unconsciously, enter into our hearts and minds and inform our thoughts, emotions and behaviors. We must ensure, to the best of our ability, that we look at objects, media, people and events that enhance our lives and cultivate good and noble thoughts, feelings and actions.

As much as possible, it is important to surround ourselves with positive, pure and expansive imagery. At home you can more easily create an environment of elevated sight. The coloring of your home, the images you hang on the walls and the overall aesthetic and ambiance should all be conducive for spiritual clarity and growth. Eliminate violent, profane or demeaning imagery wherever it may appear, whether in advertising, media or print. A home should be a safe, settled space. We need to make sure that we do not bring the turmoil and destructive energies of the outside world into our inner sanctum.

When we go out onto the street and into the world, it is important to make sure that our eyes only attach themselves to images that are definitely good for us — spiritually, mentally and emotionally. This may take courage and commitment, but every moment of positive effort creates a beneficial energy that is truly never lost.

There are Mitzvos that are connected with the mind, such as studying Torah, and there are Mitzvos connected with the hands, such as giving *Tzedakah* / charity. There are Mitzvos connected with the mouth, like reciting blessings, and there are Mitzvos connected with the eyes, like looking at one's Tzitzis or reading from *Torah ShebeKsav* / the Written Torah (*Sefer Chareidim*, Chapter 10. See also: *Medrash Tehilim* [also known, as *Medrash Shochar Tov*] Chap 35:2).

What is 'below' mirrors what is 'Above.' As such, the Mitzvos that are connected with our mind, hands, or eyes are rooted in the "mind," "hands" or "eyes", as it were, of the One Above (*Zohar* 2, 85b. 165b. *Tikkunei Zohar*, Tikkun 70). Every Mitzvah we do creates an *Ohr Makif* / Surrounding Light that envelops us in its protection. This is one of the 'rewards' of a Mitzvah; when we generate and reside within its Ohr Makif, we are actually sitting in *Gan Eden* / Paradise in our present life (*Nefesh haChayim*, Sha'ar 1:6. See *Zohar* 3, 86b). Each specific Mitzvah arouses the corresponding dimension Above and draws down a flow of Kedusha to that specific body part. For example, when a person gives Tzedakah with his hands, the Mitzvah arouses the Divine Hand Above and draws down a particular Kedusha, an Ohr Makif related to the hands. In the context of this chapter, not only should a person protect his or her eyes, but one should do Mitzvos that are connected with the eyes. By doing these Mitzvos with special care, one will draw down an Ohr Makif of protection to his or her eyes.

A second step in rectifying our eyes, and a more subtle level of practice, is learning to choose *how* we look at what we see. Determining *what* we see is, in a sense, a physical exercise; simply turning our head can usually accomplish this. *How* we look at things, on the other hand, is a mental and spiritual exercise which involves deeper inner resources. This practice can be called 'envisioning'.

When a pickpocket sees a holy Tzadik walking down the street, all he sees are pockets. When you are hungry, as you walk down the street, all you see is food. Essentially, what you observe on the outside is a reflection of what you are envisioning or experiencing on the inside.

Rabbi Bachya Ibn Pekudah, the author of *Chovos haLevavos* / Duties of the Heart, tells the story of a sage who was walking with his disciples when they happened upon a dead animal, the carcass of a donkey. The students were disgusted and turned away. But the teacher gently noted, "Did you notice the [beautiful] white teeth on the animal?" (*Chovos haLevavos*, Sha'ar haKeniyah, Chapter 6). The students just saw a decaying carcass, yet the sage 'envisioned' and saw the redemptive beauty within the apparent ugliness and decay.

This story is simple but profound. Everything and everyone has some sort of inner and outer beauty, even if it is hidden behind the surface appearance. The sage's base-line perspective of life was that of pervasive beauty, holiness and purity. Because that is what he wanted/decided to experience, it is actually what he experienced. In seeing beauty, he revealed his own inner beauty. The students were challenged to see or reveal the potential beauty of the moment, as they were not yet on his level. This challenge is one that we often face as well. When confronted with a 'decaying carcass' or some other negative or harmful image of life, the best solution is sometimes to cover our eyes or to look away. However, sometimes the deeper path of 'envisioning' is available to us. With practice, we can change our mode of perception and interpret, process, and re-contextualize what we see on the level of positivity and light. When we do so, we can actually refine what we see and reveal the holiness that is potentially present within every person, place or thing — depending on how we view it.

Sometimes, physically turning away from something or someone will be seen by others as rude or unkind. This could cause a *Chilul Hashem* / defiling of Hashem's Name in the world. If so, and you *must* assess each situation, instead of turning away, you may need to go inward and change *how* you are seeing, rather than changing *what* you are seeing. This is the practice of 'envisioning'.

As we train ourselves in the art of 'envisioning', the objects of our vision will begin to have a more positive effect upon us, regardless of what they are. We will also begin to develop a stronger and more adaptive spiritual 'immune system'. Simply looking away from things demands conviction and willpower, but 'envisioning' is much more active and requires rigorous inner training, a refined imagination and an unshakable faith in the Infinite Oneness of Hashem.

The first step in 'envisioning' is to learn to see things as they are. This requires peeling away the actual image from the thought-narratives attached to it. To illustrate this point: a person sees a shiny, new car driving down the street. Besides seeing the car itself, the person experiences some narrative that they superimpose on the car: 'I would love to own such a car.' 'I'm sure I will never own such a car.' 'The driver looks so arrogant.' 'What an irritating color.' Any desire or dissonance that arises when one sees the car is not actually coming from the car itself, but rather from the thoughts, associations and narratives projected onto it by the seer themselves. To separate a real image from its imposed narrative requires noticing your thoughts and putting them aside. Ask yourself, 'What am I thinking, and what am I actually seeing?'

The second step is to see the Divine goodness within the particular person, place or thing that you are seeing. This requires an active seeking out and uncovering of any aspect of hidden holiness, beauty or blessing within what you are looking at. Ask yourself: What might be Hashem's deeper purpose in creating this thing? How is the goodness of the Creator revealed through this phenomenon? Thank Hashem for that unique revelation of light, and focus on it.

When you look at people, practice letting go of your limited judgments and desires in relation to them. Then, envision and see the highest goodness and holiness within each person. If you see this person has something you do not have, thank Hashem that they have it. See yourself as having everything you need. This will help you overcome subtle and petty jealousies, which are rooted in one's unconscious tendencies to see things negatively, as we explored at length above.

These practices of seeing are part of the *Avodah* / spiritual work of this month, which is essentially nothing less than the elevation of the fallen sparks of holiness through active envisioning and revealing of the *Nekudah Tovah* / point of goodness within every created thing, within the world, within every person and within your own life.

ϓ

SUMMARY OF TAMUZ

THE 12 DIMENSIONS OF TAMUZ

12 Dimensions of Tamuz	
Sequence of Hashem's Name	Hei-Vav, Hei-Yud (reversal)
Torah Verse	*ZeH einenO shoveH liY*/ This is worthless to me...." (*Megilas Ester*, 5:13)
Letter	Ches (ח)
Month Name	*Tamuz* (weeping idol)
Sense	*Yirah* / Seeing
Zodiac	*Sartan* / the Crab or Cancer
Tribe	Reuven
Body Part	Right Hand
Element	*Mayim* / Water
Parshiyos	Shelach, Korach, Chukas, and Balak (each of these deals with *Ayin haRa*)
Season	Hottest Month of Summer
Holiday	17th of Tamuz

SUMMARY

*I*n the month of Tamuz, the intense heat of the summer **season** can stimulate energies of jealousy. We are thus called to make a Tikkun on jealousy in this month by rectifying our **sense** of sight and the way we view the world and others. To create this Tikkun, we employ the right hand (the **body part** of the month), which symbolizes Chesed, to point out the goodness and spiritual light within all people and situations.

The **name** of the month is also the name of a pagan idol that evoked bitter tears of jealousy. This teaches us that we need to elevate our tears — transforming the Dead Sea of Salt into fresh and living waters, the **element** of the month. Tears shed in jealousy or despondency cloud one's vision of life, while tears shed in faith and hope cleanse and clarify one's vision. The **Torah portions** of the month instruct us in this elevation, guiding us to focus on what is redemptive in life. The challenges present in this higher way of seeing the world are intensified on this month's 'holiday' of mourning, the 17th of Tamuz. Despite the great tragedies that occurred on this day, the numerical value of 17 is *Tov* / goodness. When we complete the Tikkun on our destructive views and tendencies, we will see and reveal the goodness hidden within the 17th of Tamuz, and all the light hidden within apparent darkness. Ches, the **letter** of the month, stands for *Choshech* / darkness. Yet, Ches also has a numerical value of 8, alluding to the potential Messianic Light hidden within what appears to us as darkness.

Sartan / Cancer, the Crab is the **sign** of the month. Crabs crawl sideward, alluding to a human tendency to side-step spiritual needs and feelings of sadness and suffering. The Tikkun for this unconscious avoidance is to squarely face our suffering and exile, and reveal the hidden Redemption from within them. The name of the **tribe** of the month alludes to this very dynamic: *Reuven* means, 'my suffering is seen', meaning that: it is both seen and seen-through.

The **letter sequence of Hashem's Name** for this month is a complete reversal of the proper flow of the Name, expressing deep harshness and concealment of Divine light and presence. The **verse** from which this sequence is derived expresses words of destructive jealousy uttered by Haman in Megillas Esther. In that story, when the danger of imminent destruction was courageously faced, the harsh decree was reversed. The harshness of Tamuz will be fully reversed when Redemption is revealed and seen by all. The following practice is a step toward revealing the Light of Redemption in the present moment of our personal lives.

KAVANAH: 'WHY DID I SEE THAT?'

The foundation of transforming how we look at the world is to recognize that everything we see, even if it's not our choice, we see for a deeper purpose. When we see something, it may stimulate self-centered desire or anger, but at the core of our seeing, and even of our reactions, is an energy of purity and Divine purpose.

For example, you see a nice pair of shoes, and you crave them, even though you objectively do not need another pair of shoes. The fact that you saw them and had this particular emotional reaction is teaching you something about yourself. It is a subtle Divine hint about what you are actually missing or needing in your life — and it is almost certainly not the pair of shoes. Perhaps you haven't been envisioning or cultivating your own inner beauty, creativity or nobility. Perhaps you don't see yourself as having enough. Perhaps you are not noticing the newness all around you, and so you are trying to manufacture newness by acquiring objects. Perhaps you need to work on changing your base-line perception of this Divine Creation and of your place and significance within it.

We should always meditate on what we can learn from what we see and how we react to it. How can what we see help us manifest our deepest self, be a stronger channel of blessing for others and live in closer intimacy with Hashem?

Sit quietly. Recall a time when you perceived a fault or failure within someone else.

In your mind's eye, envision yourself seeing this person. What do you look like as you look at them?

To see fault or failure, you must believe in the existential reality of faults or failures. How does that feel?

Ask yourself, "Why did I see what I saw?" "Why did I interpret what I saw in that way?" Do not try to answer these questions intellectually, just sit with the inquiry for a while.

Now ask yourself, "What is a similar 'fault', defect in character or failure that I have within me that has allowed me to see these traits or behaviors as negative within the other?"

If you consider deeply and honestly the possibility that you have blamed, looked down on and maybe even hurt others *only because of your own projected beliefs*, you may be moved to tears. If so, let them flow and cleanse your eyes, both physically and spiritually.

When you are ready, 'envision' the sparks of goodness and righteousness within the other person. See how they were doing the best they could in that moment. See how all along they were a messenger of Hashem sent to wake you up and strengthen your faith in the Infinite Oneness of Hashem.

Thank Hashem for allowing you to transform Din into Chesed.

Why do we see what we see? The world is our mirror; it is simply a reflection of who we are. Whatever we are seeing at any moment reflects back to us the inner work and *Tikkun* that we need to achieve at any given moment.

PART 2:

༃

The Month of Av

LONGING FOR UNITY & THE ART OF DEEP LISTENING

Transforming Separation into Unity Through Transcendent Listening

*A*s Above, so Below. The physical realm is a reflection of the spiritual. Av is the second of the summer months, and like Tamuz, the uncomfortable heat of Av is a reflection of the harsh spiritual nature of this month. Yet, as the days begin to get slightly shorter towards the end of the month, the summer heat begins to break. On a spiritual level, the second half of Av is therefore less intense. The month of Av is divided into two distinct qualities. The first ten days are characterized by mourning the destructions of the First and the Second Temples specifically, and all destructions of life and value in general throughout history, including the present. The second half of the month is a period of connection, healing and unity, beginning with Tu b'Av, potentially one of the most joyous days of the year.

As we saw, Tamuz is connected with the quality of 'jealousy', and Av is connected with *Ta'avah* / insatiable desire. For this reason, Tamuz and Av are joined sequentially and in their overarching themes of destruction and mourning, as jealousy and desire go hand in hand.

Hot weather can stimulate desire and lust. In Av, the summer heat is in full force, and we need to take this opportunity to direct our desires toward healthy ends. When necessary, we may even need to sublimate, elevate or transform our desires. In the month of Av we are offered a special *Koach* / strength to refine and elevate our desires to their roots, and ultimately to create a Tikkun for all of our misplaced energy and attention.

The 'insatiable desire' of Av, the fifth month of spring/summer, is the counterpoint and opposite of the 'satisfaction' of Shevat, which is the fifth month of autumn/winter. The eventual trajectory of uncontrolled desire is a life of deep dissatisfaction, strife and restlessness. By traversing this month with knowledge and intentionality, we can achieve a new level of deep listening which ultimately gives us the ability to elevate our desires and connect them to their transcendent Source.

During the first part of Av, we mourn and commemorate destruction, separation and exile, both on a collective and a personal level. We sensitize ourselves to the apparent distance and absence of the Divine. We acknowledge our separation from our homeland and our spiritual imperfection. In this consciousness of *Cheser /* lack, the desire for love and connection with others is augmented. The second half of the month commences with a festive day of courting, 'finding love', and meeting soulmates.

In the Torah's description of 'Day Two' of Creation, the word *Tov /* good does not appear, as it does on all the other days in this sequence. This is because it is the day when Hashem was separating the upper waters from the lower waters, and the land from the water. Day Two thus represents the paradigm of Divine absence, separation, deficiency and duality.

On Day Two, *Gehenom /* purgatory was created (*Medrash Rabba*, Bereishis, 4:6. *Pesachim*, 54b). *Gehenom* is a state of incompleteness (*Tiferes Yisrael*, Chap. 18), a reality of *Cheser /* absence; specifically, the apparent absence of Hashem's light. All argumentation, friction and tension were also created on this day. All of this separation is lacking *Tov*. On the other hand, in the description of Day Three, the word *Tov* appears twice: once for Day Two and once for Day Three (*Medrash Rabba*, Bereishis, 4:6). If the construct of Day Two — and two-ness in general — is so negative, what is the meaning of the displaced description of 'good'?

Separation can be good when it creates a deeper desire to reunite. On Day Two, when the lower waters were separated from the upper waters, the lower waters felt pangs of separation from the light of 'Above' and cried out, "We too want to be in the presence of the King!" (*Tikunei Zohar*, 19:2). Because of this yearning, the lower waters merited to be poured onto the altar during the Festival of Sukkos, and would thereby return to the heights as an offering (*Ramban, Rabbeinu Bachya*, Vayikra 2:13). Absence makes the heart grow fonder. The lower waters crying and desiring to be 'higher' and closer to the King is the 'good' that was brought about through the previous separation.

The contemplation of *Cheser* and destruction in the first half of the month, accompanied by the fasting and practices of collective and individual mourning, are all forms of yearning to rise and return to the presence of the Divine King.

On a personal and developmental level, 'good' refers to our positive inclinations and qualities. *Tov Me'od* / very good, however, refers to death, our negative qualities and our *Yetzer haRa* / our propensity and inclination for selfishness (*Medrash Rabba*, Bereishis 9:7). This is because the place of our deepest deficiency is the very place from which our true greatness can emerge. Our greatest accomplishments in life are catalyzed by overcoming our *Cheserim* / deficiencies and our most difficult inner challenges. When we yearn and grow from our lack, our Cheser becomes our true *Sheleimus* / completion. It is thus revealed to be very 'good'.

There are 365 negative Mitzvos or 'prohibitions' in the Torah, corresponding to the 365 days of the year (*Makos*, 23b). These also correspond to the 365 principal veins and arteries of the body (*Zohar* 1, p. 170b), and each of them is a conduit of a specific energy. The day of Tisha b'Av corresponds to the *Gid haNasheh* / sciatic nerve, and the Mitzvah to not eat this nerve (*Zohar* 1. p. 70b).

In the sentence, "Therefore the Children of Israel do not eat *Es Gid haNasheh* / the dislodged vein", the word *Es* / the (spelled Aleph-Tav) is a reversed acronym for *Tisha Av* / the Ninth of Av (*Akeidas Yitzchak*, Vayishlach, Sha'ar 26). Furthermore, the numerical value of the words *Es Gid haNasheh* is the same as the words *Tisha b'Av* (R. Pinchas of Koretz, *Imrei Pinchas*, p. 7).

The Gid haNasheh is a part of the animal that we do not eat; rather, we must remove it to ensure that the meat will be kosher. The Gid itself has no taste, as our Sages teach: *Ein Gidim Nosein Ta'am* / nerves do not transmit taste. The sciatic nerve represents Cheser on every level. It has a Cheser in its utility for us: we do not eat it. It has an existential Cheser: it must be eliminated. And, it has an aesthetic Cheser: it is tasteless.

In the Torah narrative, we read of a struggle between Yaakov, also called the *Ish Tamim* / complete one, and the "prince" or angel of his brother Eisav. This struggle is not mainly a physical struggle, but rather a spiritual struggle over Yaakov's identity. When the angel of Eisav "saw that he could not defeat him (Yaakov), he touched the upper joint of his thigh." As a result, Yaakov's hip joint became dislocated, and "therefore the Children of Israel do not eat *Es Gid haNasheh* / the dislodged vein" (*Bereishis*, 32:25-33).

Yaakov, the *Tam* / complete person, having been wounded, now had a Cheser, an 'incompletion' within him. Actually, the only place where the angel of Eisav was able to impair Yaakov was in the part of his body that was not yet perfect. Eisav knew that one can only affect another person negatively by contacting a place in the other which corresponds to one's own negativity. Yaakov now needed to contend with his Cheser. Yet, only through this imperfection was Yaakov able to achieve a deeper perfection.

On Tisha b'Av, in the heart of imperfection and Cheser, in the most extreme darkness and exile, the highest light and redemption is revealed (*Eicha Rabba*, 1:51). It is precisely in the place of the greatest absence and yearning that wholeness, connection, possibility and perfect unity can manifest. In fact, the reality of Moshiach is born on Tisha b'Av (Yerushalmi, *Berachos*, 2:4). Let us explore more deeply the major points of this powerful month.

PERMUTATION OF HASHEM'S NAME

*T*HE LETTER-SEQUENCE OF HASHEM'S NAME CORRESPOND-
ING to the month of Av is Hei-Vav-Yud-Hei. When the
letters of the Name of Hashem (Yud-Hei-Vav-Hei) are
in their proper sequence it is a sign of *Rachamim* / revealed Divine
compassion, and when the sequence of the letters are in the reverse
order, it is a sign of *Din* / judgment and concealment (*Zohar* 2, 51b).
The first part of this month corresponds to the letters Hei-Vav,
which are in reverse sequence, alluding to the Din and negativity
present in the first half of Av. The second part of the month corresponds to the letters Yud-Hei.*

---

* The vowels in the sequence of Hashem's Name for the month of Av are
Cholam-Hei, silent Vav, Kametz-Yud, silent Hei. In an alternate version according to the *Mishnas Chasidim*, the vowels are Patach-Hei, Kubutz-Vav, Chirik-Yud
and Patach-Hei.

Here, the order flows correctly, alluding to the great compassion and positivity that manifests on a revealed level from the 15ᵗʰ through the end of the month.

This four-letter sequence is the same spelling of the Name of Hashem that appears in Kabbalistic and Chassidic texts: *Ha-Va-Ya-H*. However, the vowels that accompany the letter formation of the month are different. The Hei takes the vowel *Cholam* / 'o,' which is hosted by the Vav. The Yud takes the vowel *Kamatz* / ah, and the final Hei is silent. Therefore, the pronunciation of this letter sequence would be *H-O-Ya-H*.

In the Haftorah that we read on the Shabbos preceding the Ninth of Av, when we commemorate the destruction of the Temple and our exile, the word *Hoy* means 'oy' or 'woe!'*(Yeshayahu* 1:4). The letter Hei often symbolizes the Divine Presence within Creation. Therefore, the letter-sequence H-O-Y-H (*hoy* plus Hei) suggests 'the Woe of the Divine Presence' or the suffering of the Shechinah in exile, which is the source and root of all exiles in this world.

Nevertheless, as we mentioned, our letter sequence also spells *Ha-Va-Ya-H* — a representation of the Name of Infinite Compassion.*

---

* The letter order of the month is Hei-Vav-Yud-Hei. Hei-Vav is the reverse of the normal order, and demonstrates Din and *Arur* / curse. This pertains to the first part of the month, the first 14 days. The second part of the month corresponds to the Yud-Hei, corresponding to the 15th of the month (Yud/10, Hei/5). From this point, Chesed and Beracha are revealed. The name of the month, A"v, is an acronym for *Arur*, [then] *Beracha.* (*Kedushas Levi,* Nachamu; Note *Bnei Yissachar,* Tamuz/Av, Ma'amar 1:1). Fourteen is Yud-Dalet or *Yad,* meaning 'hand'. During the first 14 days of Av, the hand of Kelipa destroyed the Beis haMikdash (*Zohar* 2, 172a; Note, *Ta'anis,* 29a). The liturgy of Mussaf recited on Festivals mentions a "hand" that was "sent upon Your Mikdash". *Pri Eitz Chayim,* Sha'ar Mikra Ko-

If we 'listen' deeply to the resonance of this month, we can hear the presence of Divine Compassion hidden even within the 'woe'.

☾

---

desh 3. Also, there will come a time when we will "Let those redeemed by Hashem tell their story, those He redeemed from the 'hand' of the foe". *Tehilim*, 107:2. All of these allude to the 'hand' of Kelipa that destroyed the Beis haMikdash.

ຈ

TORAH VERSE

CCORDING TO THE TIKUNEI ZOHAR, THE VERSE connected with this month is *Hinei Yad Hashem Hoyah* / Behold, the hand of Hashem is upon… (*Shemos*, 9:3). The verse speaks of the Plague of *Dever*, or the 'epidemic' that killed the domestic animals of Egypt, and thereby brought *Din* upon the Egyptians. This symbolizes the harsh 'judgment' in the first part of Av. However, by means of the Plagues, the Egyptians were eventually able to recognize the Oneness of Hashem. The intention behind Divine Judgment is always a greater revelation of Divine Compassion. Similarly, the quality of judgment in the beginning of Av is *eventually* revealed to be for the good. The second part of the month is a *direct* revelation of Divine Compassion.

The letter combination of the month is derived from the last word in the verse, *Hoyah* / is — the present-tense status of being. (The spelling of this word is Hei-Vav-Yud-Hei, and thus means *Hoveh* / present tense *Rashi*, ibid.) It is very unusual that a letter sequence is derived not from the first or last letters of four different words, but rather from a single word; this phenomenon invites attention and interpretation. As we mentioned above, *Hoyah* can also mean 'woe.' As an indicator of the present tense, the word directs our attention to the woe and the Din that is present for us even now. On Tisha b'Av, we meditate on our historical sufferings as symbols for contemporary sufferings. Being 'present' with suffering as it arises is the first step in transforming it into compassion. Similarly, in the English word 'compassion', *com* means 'present with' and *passion* means 'suffering'.

Alternatively, the Mishnas Chasidim and others, teach that the verse of the month (from which the same letter combination is derived) is *Hashkes U-shema Yisrael Hayom* / Keep silent and hear Israel, today (*Devarim*, 27:9). "Keep silent and hear" means to listen deeply and allow the words of the speaker to penetrate your heart. As we will explore, the month of Av is connected with deep listening, and hearing what is concealed from surface perception.

ט

LETTER

*T*HE LETTER OF THE MONTH IS TES (ט).THE ESSENTIAL meaning of a given letter is expressed in the first word appearing in the Torah which begins with that letter. The first place Tes appears in the Torah is as the first letter of *Tov* (*Bereishis*, 1:4). Tes thus stands for *Tov* / good. Because of this first appearance, if a person sees the letter Tes in his dreams, it is a 'good sign' (*Baba Kama*, 55a).

Interestingly, Tes is the least common letter in the entire Torah. From among all the 22 letters, Tes is thus the most 'concealed' letter. In fact, all the letters are mentioned in the first set of Luchos, except for the letter Tes (*Ibid*, see also: *Pesikta Zutrasa*, Devarim 9b). This is because Tes represents concealment, specifically, 'concealed good'.

According to the Zohar, the shape of Tes ט turns inward, hinting at the *Tov haGanuz* / Hidden Goodness that is enfolded within our worldly reality.*

---

* Tes represents 'hidden goodness'. In 13ᵗʰ Century Castile there were two prominent *Mekubalim* / kabbalists, Rabbi Yaakov haKohen and his brother Rabbi Yitzchak haKohen. Rabbi Yaakov wrote a commentary on the letters of the Torah. On the letter Tes he writes that the graphic design of the letter Tes is a Pei connected to a Zayin. Pei and Zayin spell the word *Paz* / finest gold, and have a numerical value of 87 (*Sefer Amudei haKabalah*, Kabbalas R. Yitzchak, R. Yaakov, p. 16). This numerical value is hidden within each letter of the Torah, as their deepest core. We will describe this phenomenon below.

Everything is composed of four basic nested elements. There is also a hidden fifth element which is called the *Yuli* / core potential. To identify this inner potential within each letter, let us combine the hidden inner center of each letter with the center of that center, and the center of that center, down to five center-points.

'ALEPH' is spelled *Aleph, Lamed, Pei.*
1. The center letter above is Lamed, which equals 30.
2. The center letter of Lamed (spelled Lamed, Mem, Dalet) is Mem = 40.
3. The center letter of Mem (which can be spelled Mem, Yud, Mem) is Yud = 10.
4. The center letter of Yud (spelled Yud, Vav, Dalet) is Vav = 6.
5. The center letter of Vav (which can be spelled Vav, Aleph, Vav) is Aleph = 1.
The combination of these five center-points, 30+40+10+6+1 = 87 (*Paz*).

'BEIS' is spelled *Beis, Yud, Tav.*
1. The center letter above is Yud = 10.
2. The center letter of Yud (spelled *Yud, Vav, Dalet*) is Vav = 6.
3. The center letter of Vav (which can be spelled *Vav, Aleph, Vav*) is Aleph = 1.
4. The center letter of Aleph (spelled *Aleph, Lamed, Pei*) is Lamed = 30.
5. The center letter of Lamed (spelled *Lamed, Mem, Dalet*) is Mem = 40.
The combination of these five center-points, 10+6+1+30+40 = 87 (*Paz*).

'GIMEL' is spelled *Gimel, Yud, Mem, Lamed.*
1. There are four letters above, so we can choose either the Yud or the Mem. Mem = 40.

In this way, Av is actually a 'good' month. The negativity of the first nine days is only due to the concealment of that ever-present goodness.

The letter Tes is shaped like a womb. We could say that the great goodness hidden within this month is like an unborn baby hidden within the womb of its mother, just waiting to be revealed. *Tes* is also the numeral 9, hinting at the hidden goodness within the Ninth of Av. Indeed, we learn that on the Ninth of Av, the soul of Moshiach is 'born', meaning that the *Tov haGanuz* begins to emerge from the womb of concealment and manifest in the world on a new level.

---

2. The center letter of Mem (which can be spelled *Mem, Yud, Mem*) is Yud = 10.

3. The center letter of Yud (spelled *Yud, Vav, Dalet*) is Vav = 6.

4. The center letter of Vav (which can be spelled *Vav, Aleph, Vav*) is Aleph = 1.

5. The center letter of Aleph (spelled *Aleph, Lamed, Pei*) is Lamed = 30.

The combination of these five center-points, 40+10+6+1+30 = 87 (*Paz*).

'DALET' is spelled *Dalet, Lamed, Tav*.

1. The center letter above is Lamed = 30.

2. The center letter of Lamed (spelled *Lamed, Mem, Dalet*) is Mem = 40.

3. The center letter of Mem (which can be spelled *Mem, Yud, Mem*) is Yud = 10.

4. The center letter of Yud (spelled Yud, Vav, Dalet) is Vav = 6.

5. The center letter of Vav (which can be spelled Vav, Aleph, Vav) is Aleph = 1.

The combination of these five center-points, 30+40+10+6+1 = 87 (*Paz*).

This method works with all 22 letters of the Aleph-Beis!

Thus, the hidden essence of every letter, word, and description in the Torah is *Paz*, the 'finest gold', which is also the hidden Tes or 'Goodness'.

The 'hidden good' is synonymous with the *Tov Me'od* / very good, as mentioned in the introduction to the month of Av, above. This is the goodness that is revealed in the seeming absence of goodness; in *Cheser* / deficiency, in death and in the *Yetzer haRa*. It is a goodness that is revealed precisely through the mechanism of absence (*Chasam Sofer*, Derush Zayin, Av). The revelation of hidden goodness is triggered when the challenges in our lives stimulate an acute awareness and strong yearning within us to reach out and reconnect directly to goodness and positivity.

Based on the examples above, we can see that in general Tes represents something (goodness) hidden. In fact, there is a tradition that the ninth (Tes) verse in every Parsha of the Torah has a much deeper meaning than how it appears on the surface (*Mei haShiloach*, Parshas Balak and Parshas Devarim). 'Hiddenness' is also related to the sense of hearing, the sense of this month. When we see something we can apprehend all of it immediately; with one glance the entire picture is revealed. However, when it comes to sound, we are only able to hear something bit by bit; at any given moment, most of the sounds are 'hidden', waiting to be revealed in sequence.

As mentioned in the last chapter, the letter Tes from this month, plus the letter Ches from the previous month of Tamuz, together spell *Cheit* / missing the mark or sin. Av is a time when the negativity of our *Cheit* comes to the surface in order to be 'heard' and healed; it is therefore a time of harsh judgment.

Tes is the ninth letter of the Aleph-Beis, and is thus a symbol for the number 9. This is one of the numerical values of the word *Emes* / truth or eternity (Aleph/1 + Mem/4[0] + Tav/ 4[00] = 9). 9

is eternally 'true' to itself; when 9 is multiplied by any number, the digits in the product always add up to 9 (for example, 9 x 3 = 27, and 2 + 7 = 9). According to the Zohar, Tes is a symbol for eternity (*Zohar* 2, p. 151b-152a), or the eternal goodness hiding behind every appearance.

Tes and *Tov* are hidden within the first nine days of Av. This is the Cheser and alienation felt during these days, which serve to create a strong yearning for the opposite, helping to reveal an outward manifestation of the goodness and fulfilment hidden within such harsh times.

NAME OF THE MONTH

EFORE THE BABYLONIAN EXILE, THIS MONTH WAS simply called 'the Fifth Month', as we find in the Torah regarding the date of Aharon's death: "Aaron the priest went up to Mount Hor, where he died on the first day of the fifth month of the 40th year after the Israelites came out of Egypt. (*Bamidbar*, 33:38)" It is important to note that the mention of this month in the Torah is connected to death, the death of Aaron. In fact, our Sages call this month "the month that Aaron the priest passed away" (*Sanhedrin*, 12a). Correspondingly, Av is the month that we embrace the Cheser, absence, and death in our lives and in our history, as will be explored shortly.

After the Exile, this month was called 'Av.' The word *Av* apparently comes from the Akkadian name for the month, *Abu*, meaning 'hostile'. Av is known as a spiritually 'hostile' month, as it is the month in which both Temples were destroyed. *Av* (spelled Aleph-Beis) is an acronym for *Edom-Bavel* / Rome-Babylon. These are the two empires that destroyed the Temples — the First Temple by the Babylonians and the Second by the Romans.

In Hebrew, *Av* literally means 'father.' In ancient Sumerian, the name of the fifth month is *Ab-ba*, which in Hebrew also means 'father'.

The laws of *Gittin* / divorce indicate that the Halachic name of this month is *Av*, and must be written as such in legal documents (*Kav Naki*, 51:4). However, when we bless the new moon of Av, and also when we write a *Kesubah* / marriage contract, we use the name *Menachem Av*. This name means 'the Consolation of Av', 'the Consolation of the Father' or 'the Consoling Father'. This shows that the deeper reality of the month is goodness, the hidden goodness of a loving father consoling his beloved children after a hostile and traumatic experience.

When the letters of a word are in the same order as they appear in the Hebrew Aleph-Beis, it is generally a sign of Divine Compassion. *Av* (again, spelled *Aleph-Beis*) is a prime example of this dynamic, as it is comprised of the first two letters of the *Aleph-Beis* arranged in their natural forward-flowing order. By contrast, Tishrei, the month of the High Holy Days, is spelled *Tav-Shin-Reish*. These are the last three letters of the Aleph-Beis in reverse order, demonstrating the quality of *Din* / judgment that is present during that month.

We see that, despite appearances, the month of Av is a month of Divine Compassion and consolation. *Av* is like a father who is *Menachem*, 'bringing consolation' to us, despite the surface tension and general atmosphere of hostility within the month. On a deeper level, the disturbing events in the first third of Av remind us of a father who rebukes his child out of love and compassion (RaShaB, *Sefer haMa'amarim*, Eter, p. 218, *Nachamu*). 'Hearing' rebuke truly means to be receptive to the positive, holy, loving and life-affirming intention behind the critique, as the verse says, "My son, hear the *Musar* / rebuke of your father" (*Mishlei*, 1:8).

When we recognize that our suffering or rebuke is given to us by a caring parent in order to motivate our growth, we can sense a deeper consolation hidden within it. This is because growth is what we truly crave, beneath all of our gripes and complaints. Growth is the potential goodness hidden within our deficiencies and insatiable desires.

☽

SENSE

'HEARING' IS THE SENSE OF THE MONTH. HEARING occurs through a gradual process; to hear a full sentence requires deciphering sounds, understanding context, gaining insight and relating information to prior knowledge. Hearing occurs one bit of information at a time, culminating in a summation within your mind of the entire sentence, as the verse says, "*vayiShama Shaul* / And Saul (heard) called the people together" (*Shmuel* I, 15:4); hearing is thus a process of 'bringing together' the separate words and sounds into a cohesive sentence. *Churban* / destruction is the breaking apart of reality; the opposite of Churban is *Chaver* / friend or connection (they have the same root letters). The historical Churban of the Temple is the breaking apart of the spiritual reality of the Temple and the root of our exile from our land, which is essentially a breaking apart of our relationship with our homeland. When there is a breakdown in our sense of hearing, and we are not able to 'bring things together' and be in a place of unity, we experience Churban. This is one reason why this month is connected to the sense of hearing.

Hearing also has an amazing spiritual power. The deepest truths in the world are revealed through our spiritual 'sense of hearing', bringing us to an awareness of realities beyond what the eyes can see. In the future, when the inner sense of hearing will be utterly transformed, we will be able to "see" what now we can only hear. The Torah says, *Shema Yisrael* / Listen O Israel, and *v'Hayah Im Shamo'a* / and it will be if you will listen.... In these verses, the Torah wants us to apprehend the truth of Hashem's Unity through mindful listening and conscious contemplation. Although we do not yet 'see' the Presence of Hashem in this world, we can 'listen' deeply and thereby recognize it bit by bit. When we 'hear' and decipher the hints of Divine Presence in our lives, we can gradually gain deeper insight into the true nature of the world. Finally, in the Messianic era we will be able to piece together the full 'sentence' of Hashem's ever-present Compassion, composed of the shattered sparks of Creation scattered to the four corners and brought back together in our refined consciousness.

Lack of listening causes breakdowns in communication, which can lead to the destruction of relationships. The *Meraglim* / spies that Moshe sent to observe the Land of Israel, were in the Land during Tamuz (See our chapter on Tamuz), and returned to report to the people what they saw on the Ninth of Av. However, there was a communication breakdown; the people were not really listening to the report, but instead listening to their own defeatist inner narratives. This led them to disbelieve in their ability to enter the Land, and they wept as a result of this loss of faith. This is how the Ninth of Av became a day of weeping. Because we wept on that day without reason, eventually the Ninth of Av became a day of national mourning (*Ta'anis,* 29a).

The sense associated with Tamuz, the previous month, is *Re'iya* / seeing. The first letters of *Rei'ya* and *Shemi'a,* Reish and Shin, spell *Rosh* / poor. This is a time of poverty, as it were. Similarly, as explored in the previous chapter, the words *Tamuz* and *Av* are also connected with the word *Dal* / poverty or lack. When the four letters in the Divine Name *Adon-ai* are themselves spelled out, they unfold into twelve letters corresponding to the twelve months of the year (Aleph=Aleph-Lamed-Pei, Dalet=Dalet-Lamed-Tav, Nun=Nun-Vav-Nun, Yud=Yud-Vav-Dalet). The fourth and fifth letters, corresponding to Tamuz and Av, are Dalet and Lamed, spelling the word *Dal.* During these two months, we feel the weight of our spiritual, ethical and existential poverty. Yet, it is precisely when we are most powerless and empty that our highest potential can be birthed and revealed.

On the 15th of Av, in ancient Israel, women who wanted to get married would go out into the fields, dressed in anonymous white garments. As the unmarried men would approach, the women would call to them, *Bachur, Sa Na Einecha* / Young man, lift your eyes (*Ta'anis,* 26b). In other words, the men would first 'listen' to their future brides and only then lift their eyes and 'see' who had called to them. This was part of the Tikkun for the negative, impulsive 'seeing' of Tamuz. It was as well a Tikkun for the negative types of 'hearing' connected to Av, such as listening to the unfavorable report of the *Meraglim.*

From the 15th of Av on, we are given heightened abilities to listen deeply and to connect with others. It is therefore a time when one can find lasting love; as genuine love flourishes in an atmosphere of deep listening. When we listen to our spouse, children, family or community, and respond with sensitivity and respect, we can fix what is broken. We can build stronger vessels of love, of unity and of healing.

The Parallel Twenty One Days

There are 21 days from the 17th of Tamuz until Tisha b'Av. This period parallels the 21 days from Rosh Hashanah until Hoshana Rabbah. Together, these two periods comprise 42 days. This number reminds us of the 42 journeys of the Children of Israel in the Desert, corresponding to the '42' spiritual journeys we experience in our own lives, from 'slavery' to 'freedom' and beyond. If we meditate and take on appropriate spiritual practices, we can actively transform the Nine Days of Av into an inner journey moving us out from the ruins of our history into a bright, new future of hope and Redemption.

In the summer, people are prone to go outdoors and interact more freely, spending time with both friends and strangers. People often travel, and so they 'see' and 'hear' a variety of new things, alluding, again, to the two senses of Tamuz and Av. In both cases, people are more vulnerable to the impressions that others seem to have of them.

Negative hearing is, metaphorically, to listen to the 'advice of the spies' who say "...and there we saw giants...and we were in our own eyes as grasshoppers, and so were we in their eyes" (*Bamidbar*, 13:33). In their view of themselves, they were inferior and unfit for the task at hand. Believing in the opinions of others who put you down is the most intense form of slavery or *Kelipah* / inner self-concealment. The Tikkun for listening to such 'bad advice' is to hear the hidden good in what others say. This is one way to journey toward greater spiritual freedom, and to transform alienating pain into love and connection.

We need to listen to the right people, and also open ourselves up to listen deeply to the people that are close to us. There are people in our lives who need us to hear them, and what's more, they need to hear us respond to them with goodness and respect. When we do this, we can heal brokenness, and build stronger vessels of love, unity and understanding all around us.

The Art of Listening

Deep listening includes listening to what another is really trying to say, not merely what you want to hear. Deep listening is by definition free of such anxious craving to respond, even before the other has finished speaking.

The ability to share our thoughts, feelings and ideas with others is a soul quality given to each of us. It is an ability to leave our personal space and enter into another person's space through the vehicle of words. But to listen to another person, to become the container and receiver of another person's life story, is even deeper; it emulates the Divine quality of radical receptivity and unconditional presence.

Like all arts, deep listening has to be cultivated and practiced. The more we practice listening, the more proficient and present we become. In order to cultivate listening, and to create a Tikkun in the manner in which we listen, it helps to have a map. We will now explore ten levels of listening, within four subcategories: physical, intellectual, soulful and transcendent. Each subcategory represents a deeper level of openness and unity in relationship with the other person.

Physical Hearing

1) *Passive non-listening* is physical hearing at its most rudimentary level. Our ears are open, but we are apathetic and indifferent to the other person's words. Sadly, this robotic kind of listening is the default mode in our times, when we are absorbed in multitasking or using our phones and devices for many hours a day.

2) *Active non-listening* is deliberately ignoring the words spoken by others and actively rejecting information that we hear. As a chosen response, this may have value in certain situations. If someone is insulting you, or you are in a situation where you cannot avoid negative speech by walking away, it might be beneficial to simply block it out.

3) *Pretending* is showing outward signs of listening, but inwardly blocking or rejecting what is being heard. Again, this type of listening may be useful, as when someone is speaking meaningless words at you without restraint. On the other hand, if they are reaching out to you, you might be able to help them by listening to what is unsaid.

4) *Recording* is listening in order to mechanically accumulate the information being heard. This is similar to the inanimate functioning of a recording device or the rote memorization of a young student. In this case there is still no real connection or relationship between speaker and listener, or to the meaning of the message.

On these levels, real listening is stunted by the static of self-centered judgment, anxiety or disinterest. There is no real relationship yet between the speaker and the listener.

II. Mental Hearing

5) *Projecting* is hearing what you want to hear, rather than what the other person really has to say. Information is received, and you are actively listening, but the information is filtered through your own mental static or self-centered beliefs and then projected upon the speaker. You are not really listening to the other, you are merely listening to yourself and attributing it to the other.

6) *Manipulating* is deliberately and even maliciously 'hearing what you want to hear'. Whereas *projecting* is more passive or unconscious, in *manipulating*, the listener actively twists what the other says for self-centered purposes. It goes without saying that this can destroy a personal relationship.

The above levels belong to an 'i-it' paradigm of relationship in which the listener objectifies the speaker as an object or an 'it'. As a result, the listener often tries to give the speaker advice, to fix the 'it' or to appear more wise than the 'it'. This is actually speaking rather than listening. On the higher levels of listening detailed below, there is no offering of advice. However, when you are really listening, the person speaking to you becomes empowered to 'hear' answers and truly helpful 'advice' arising within himself. He may even be able to draw from your strength and wisdom to find answers, if need be.

If the speaker is sincerely asking for your advice, you need to first be certain that you are listening on the higher levels. Then, only after pausing to internalize their issue and make it your own, should you offer advice.

III. Soulful Hearing

7) *Real Hearing* is listening without the static, projection or manipulation characterized by the levels above. To some extent, you are putting yourself aside in order to receive more deeply what the other has to say. This is the beginning of deep lis-

tening; you are receiving their story for what it is. The speaker already feels invited to share or unburden, and your mere act of listening is healing.

8) *Empathetic Listening* is being open to the other as a whole person, behind and beyond their story. This allows you to perceive and understand the subtle meanings in their intonation, gesture, body language and posture. You thereby begin to feel and respect where the other is coming from. Essentially, on this level of hearing, you are in contact with the person's soul.

This category of listening activates the "I-you" paradigm, the place of real relationship. When we step out of our own way, we can be open to the inner heart of another.

IV. Transcendental Hearing

9) *Empowering* is listening in a way that empowers the speaker's physical, mental and spiritual potential. When someone asks you for advice, you trust that the answers are already within them. By letting them tap into their own answers, you empower them to bring out their higher intuition. Both of you can begin to sense the unity between yourselves, as you are to some extent transcending the sense of separation between listener and speaker. Because you have let go of your egoic, individual self, you are able to hear the other as they are, and not just as you expect or project them to be.

10) *Unifying* is when your listening has become the speaker's

own listening. This is also called 'mutual listening', as the existential divide between listener and speaker has vanished. As a result, 'your' innate powers become manifest within the 'speaker'. For example, if you are in a calm state and the speaker has been struggling with anger, through this practice of 'unifying', your positive trait manifests spontaneously within him as well, giving him the strength to overcome anger in his life. This type of listening comes about through an authentic recognition that there is really only One Being, that every 'i' is merely an expression of the Ultimate I.

This is the 'I-I' paradigm of relationship, which transcends the relationship of separate personalities. You become 'one' with the other, without losing yourself. Losing your ego in the other person's ego would not be true 'oneness', nor would it allow you to help them in any substantial or meaningful way. In this paradigm, rather, both the speaker and the listener sense the Presence of the Ultimate 'I' of the Creator, and realize their ultimate connection through that all-encompassing Unity.

Listening to the Oneness in Creation

The Baal Shem Tov reveals the implications of listening to the Oneness in all things. He shows us that every letter or articulation of Divine Light composing Creation contains the primal dimensions of *Olamos*, *Neshamos*, and *Elokus* / worlds, souls (or angels) and Divinity. Deep listening allows you to perceive these three dimensions, simultaneously and inclusively, within any object or person. The perception of one dimension does not cancel out the presence of the others. This inter-inclusivity of microcosmic elements within every phenomenon is a revelation of the Oneness permeating all of Creation. It is therefore the inner point that we need to contact in another person, in order to hear them in the fullest sense.

Olamos / worlds is in the plural — alluding to the perception of the interconnectedness of all places and events that allows you to extrapolate through analogy what the other truly *means* by what they say. When someone is speaking to you, you are able to listen deeply and hear the 'worlds' within their words. You are able to hear where others are coming from, and what is truly bothering them or uplifting them. This is the level of *meaning*.

Neshamos / souls or angels alludes to hearing the deeper message and lesson within the other person's words. What is the Divine message and intent that is being imparted via the person that is now speaking to you? This is the level of *message*.

Elokus / Divinity alludes to recognizing and sensing that the 'I' of the speaker and the 'I' of the listener are merely expressions of the Ultimate 'I', the only actual identity of Creation. To 'hear' this is to hear the Presence of Hashem within the other person. This is the level of *monism*.

Listening to Hashem Speaking Through Another Person

We are all gifted with the ability to humbly receive the deeper story, intent and identity of another person — the *meaning*, *message* and *monism* behind everything they say. All we need to do is be present and open our heart to unifying with their heart. Within this unity of hearts, we sense the *Elokus*, the presence of Hashem there, and the *Deveikus* / unity with Hashem that underlies the relationship. This type of listening also manifests when we take the attitude that the Creator is speaking to you through the person. This can be subdivided into five levels:

Nefesh: Hear within the other person's words Hashem calling you to action.

Ruach: Hear in the other person's words the positive emotion that Hashem wants to arouse in you.

Neshamah: Hear in the other person's words the wisdom that Hashem wants to teach you.

Chayah: Hear in the other person's words the aliveness of the Divine life-force, which is the "sound of the Beloved knocking" (*Shir haShirim*, 5:2), arousing your will to unify with Hashem.

Yechidah: Hear Hashem speaking through your own words, making your words channels of Divine wisdom. In the purest expression of this, "the Shechinah was speaking through the throat of Moshe" (*Zohar* 3, Pinchas, 232). The Shechina 'speaking through

Moshe' refers to the final book of the Torah, *Devarim* / Deuteronomy, which we begin to read during the month of Av. The *Devarim* / words in this book, are Moshe's: "These are the words that Moshe spoke" (*Devarim*, 1:1), yet they are simultaneously the Divine words of the Torah. We will explore this spiritual phenomenon in more depth, shortly.

☾

♈

SIGN

*T*HE CONSTELLATION OF AV IS ARYEH / LION OR LEO. The numerical value of the word *Aryeh* is 216 (Aleph/1 + Reish/200 + Yud/10 + Dalet 4 = 216). The Nine Days of mourning in the beginning of Av comprise 216 hours (9 x 24 = 216). This is also the numerical value of the word *Gevurah*, connoting contractive 'strength' or *Din*, alluding to the intense quality of 'judgment' in these days. However, 216 is also three times the value of the word *Chesed* / kindness (*Chesed* = 72, and 3 x 72 = 216). This teaches us that there is a deeper reality of Chesed within Gevurah.*

Leo is related to fire, and the Ramak writes that the element of fire is prevalent in the month of Av (*Pardes Rimonim*, 21:16).

---

* During the Nine Days (or during the week of Tisha b'Av) we refrain from eating meat. (Red) meat is associated with the attribute of Gevurah, which is often connected with the color red. We purposefully refrain from foods connected to Gevurah during this time, and in turn, eat more (white) dairy (or fish) dishes, which are connected to Chesed, which is often connected to the color white.

Fire can be extremely constructive or extremely destructive; it can bring clear light and warmth or it can bring thick smoke and darkness. The fiery quality of Leo is manifest in *Ta'avah* / passionate desire, or craving. The *Avodah* / spiritual work of this month involves transforming our potentially destructive, dark, passionate desires into constructive forces of illumination.

Leos crave to be the center of attention, and as a result, many great world leaders have been Leos. Leos are bold determined and tend to dominate others. These character traits can ignite egoic pride and craving for dominance, or, when refined and channeled, they can fuel courageous, skillful and selfless leadership.

The Medrash says that Moshiach is "born" in Av (Yerushalmi, *Berachos*, 2:4). This future leader of Klal Yisrael, and of the entire world, is therefore a Leo. What is the Torah's definition of leadership? When Moshe is about to pass away and transfer the responsibility of leadership, Hashem tells him to choose Yehoshua since *Ruach Bo* / the Spirit is within him (*Bamidbar*, 27:18). The Ramban (*ad loc*) says that *Ruach Bo* means the person can "meet the Spirit within every individual person" (Berachos, 58a. See preface to *Tanya*). Such a person can encounter and understand the unique self within each individual person that they meet or lead.

Leadership, as above, is defined by the deepest level of listening, the 'I-I' relationship. When you listen to another person deeply, achieving a high level of unity with them without losing yourself, you are free of ego and thus your leadership or advice is most effective.

☾

⟡
TRIBE

HE TRIBE OF THE MONTH IS SHIMON, MEANING 'HEARD' (*Pirush haRavad,* Sefer Yetzirah). His mother Leah gave him this name, saying, "Since Hashem has heard that I am unloved, He has given me this one also" (*Bereishis,* 29:3). She painfully yearned for love and connection, as we do in the beginning of Av. She was eventually consoled, however, by the revelation of love that was manifest through her childbirth. We are likewise consoled by the revelations of love manifesting through the 15th of Av.

Shimon is thus connected to hearing the voice of the 'unloved' and aching heart. Shimon represents our sensitivity to those who need us to hear them, empathize and unify with them, hold their story and empower them.

Shimon is related to the level of *Sod* / secret, the hiddenness connected to the place of *Safek* / doubt, the place of uncertainty (*Mei haShiloach*, Toldos). For instance, when Yaakov is giving his *Beracha* / prophetic blessing to Shimon, he says Shimon has a "secret" (*Bereishis*, 49:6). The secret is that Shimon listens — he empathizes fully with people and connects to their places of 'doubt' — the places where they doubt if they are loveable, the places where they stumble into mistakes and depravity. In fact, the name *Shimon* has the letters of the words *Sham Aven* / there is depravity there (*Toldos Aaron*, Pinchas), alluding to his ability to listen to the darkest doubts in people. The path of Shimon is thus fraught with spiritual danger. In fact, other tribes were wary of this path, and even scared to live in close proximity to the tribe of Shimon (See *Shach Al HaTorah*, Matos, Umikna Rav). Certainly, the path of Shimon is not for the faint of heart, nor for those who are more concerned with themselves than they are with helping others. Shimon represents the Tzadik who is willing to go to the deepest depths in order to elevate those who have fallen, to the highest heights.

Through contacting those 'darker' places of 'Safek', Shimon transmits the empowering message that: it is precisely in our places of doubt that our spiritual growth and connection to Hashem can be revealed.

Shimon was the defender of his sister Dinah after she was raped. Generations later, a head of the tribe of Shimon, Zimri, became the defender of the 'sinners' of Klal Yisrael in the episode of the idolatry of Baal Peor. In this way, Shimon represents the 'hidden' way, the way of the Baal Teshuvah, the path of one who falls and gets up — much like the path and dynamic of the month of Av.

Many of the 'unnamed' Sages of the Talmud were named Shimon. Reish Lakish's name does not appear in the text since before he became a Baal Teshuvah, he was a bandit; Ben Azai and Ben Zoma's names were hidden because they did not receive official *Semichah* / ordination; Bar Kochba's name was hidden because his title eclipsed his name. In each of these cases, their real name was Shimon (see, for example, *Sanhedrin*, 17b). Shimon is thus considered a 'hidden' name. Indeed, the great revealer of the hidden wisdom, Rabbi Shimon bar Yochai, the Rashbi, is also named Shimon. And there is a mystical, 'hidden' tradition that the Rashbi is in fact from the tribe of Shimon (*Mei haShiloach*, Titzavah. R. Tzadok, *Takanans Ha-Shavim*, 6).

Beyond what the eye can see is the tribe of Shimon. Shimon represents the quality of not simply looking at what is seen in the present, but being able to hear and sense the possibility of the future. We are told that the tribe of Shimon were scribes and teachers of children (*Medrash Rabbah*, *Rashi*, Bereishis, 49:7). In many ways, both of these professions are connected with an acute sense of the 'future'. Scribes write Torahs to be read by Jewish communities in now and in the future, and teachers dedicate their time and energy to preparing children for the future. Both of these endeavors are intrinsically connected to the quality of Shimon, as they often leave the person monetarily poor in the present (Ibid), but their payoff eventually comes in a more positive and spiritually healthy future. Each of these holy professions can thus be seen as impoverishing oneself in the present for the sake of the elevation and illumination of others in the future. This is the quintessence of the path of Shimon.

꘎

BODY PART

*T*HE BODY PART ASSOCIATED WITH AV IS THE LEFT KIDNEY. The kidneys function as a filtering system, processing close to 200 quarts of blood per day, and sifting out about two quarts of waste and extra water, which eventually become urine.

This filtering and sifting function alludes to our ability to differentiate between good and it's opposite. Our Sages tell us that the kidneys give us *Eitza* / advice (*Berachos*, 61a). Rashi (*ibid*) writes that the source of this idea is in the book of *Tehilim* / Psalms: "Even at night my kidneys advise me" (16:7). According to the Maharsha (*Berachos*, *ibid*), the kidneys symbolize our ability to choose good from bad.

The left kidney is connected with the 'left-column' qualities of Gevurah, which manifest as separation and differentiation. On an intellectual level, the 'left kidney' alludes to the mind's ability to sift information and break it down into discrete units and different details. This is similar in function and process to the sense of hearing, which requires us to receive a stream of separate pieces of information. As stated earlier, hearing occurs one bit of information at a time, culminating in a summation within your mind of the entire sentence. Hearing is thus a type of bringing together of separate words and sounds into a cohesive statement. As such, before jumping to the level of cohesive comprehension, we must listen carefully and sift through what is shared with us in order to assess fully what is actually being said. This is the message and mechanism of the 'left kidney'. Furthermore, we can only give truly effective and empowering advice to others when we listen deeply to the different layers of information they are sharing, and recognize their unique qualities and potentials. This type of hearing is not merely performed with the 'ear', as it were, and thus it is not the ear that is the representative body part of the month. For this level of redemptive hearing we actually need to listen with our kidneys; we need to hear the other all the way, deep down in our *Kishkes* / innards.

☌

ELEMENT

*A*V IS THE ELEMENT OF FIRE REFLECTED IN THE passions of deep relationship, which are rooted in the realms of redemptive listening.

As noted above, fire can either be extremely constructive or extremely destructive; it can bring clear light and warmth or it can bring thick smoke and darkness. In the month of Av, we commemorate the destruction by fire of the First and Second *Batei Mikdash* / Temples. We also celebrate the constructive, illuminating and passionate aspects of fire, as Av is also the month in which Moshiach is born and Tziyon is rebuilt with holy fire (*Baba Kama*, 60b. The Nusach of *Nacheim*). This refers to a time when we will experience the 'higher fire', the fire that does not consume, destroy or take life in order to exist. Then we will experience a Temple made of 'heavenly fire' descending from Heaven (Rashi, *Rosh Hashanah*, 30a. *Sukkah* 41a. Rashi, Tosefos), which will illuminate and energize the bricks and mortar of this physical world, revealing the Infinite Light hidden within.

☾

ᘯᕈᘰ

TORAH PORTIONS

*I*N THIS FIFTH MONTH OF THE YEAR, WE BEGIN TO READ
THE fifth book of the Torah called *Devarim* or Deuteronomy. The word *Deuteronomy* is derived from the Greek word
Deuteronomion, which means Second Law. In Hebrew, this book
is also called *Mishneh Torah* / The Repetition of the Torah, as it
recounts all the major events experienced in the Desert, as well as
various laws that had already been delineated in the previous four
books (*Tosefos*, Gittin, 2a). The entire book of Devarim consists of one
very long speech that Moshe delivers during the final 37 days of
his life.

Devarim literally means 'words', referring specifically to the
words of Moshe: "These are the Devarim that Moshe spoke to all
Israel on the East Bank of the Jordan..." (*Devarim* 1:1). The earlier

books of the Torah are also transcribed by Moshe, but they are written in third person, such as in the frequently used phrase, "And Hashem spoke to Moshe, saying...." In this book, Moshe writes in the first person, frequently introducing his statements with the phrase, "Hashem spoke to me, saying...."

In a sense, throughout the first four books, Moshe was not fully present as an individual. Yet in the fifth book, Moshe speaks "in his own words" (*Megillah*, 31b). He is finally present as an individual self, even though his words are spoken with *Ruach HaKodesh* / self-less Holy Spirit (*Tosefos*, ibid).

In the Zohar, Rabbi Shimon says: "We were taught that the rebuke...in the book of Mishneh Torah was (written by) Moshe by himself. Do you think that Moshe said even one small letter by himself? No, it was written with precision...(and the words that) came from Moshe's mouth were spoken in the Voice which possessed Moshe"(*Zohar* 3, VaEschanan, 265a) — as is known, "the Shechinah was talking through the throat of Moshe" (See *Zohar* 3, 232a).

The Book of Devarim is therefore the Divine Wisdom the way it was 'heard' and unpacked by Moshe as an individual, and transmitted through his own unique voice. It expresses the way Moshe first absorbed the Divine Wisdom and then transmitted it, unlike the first four books wherein the wisdom simply passed through him. Everything has an intermediary level; whereas the Written Torah is a direct revelation from Above, the Oral dimension of the Torah (including the Mishnah, Gemara, Medrash, etc.) is an intermediary process allowing the Upper Wisdom to be accessed and assimilated by lower beings, i.e., by human intelligence. The book of Devarim is considered a bridge between the direct 'Revelation of Sinai' and the Oral Torah (*Zohar* 3, 261a), as it initiated and modeled the beginning stages of human interpretation and expression of Divine Revelation, while still being included within the 'Written Torah' itself. By means of this bridge, the Oral traditions which are passed through a chain of individuals, and their creative insights, remain consistent with the deeper intentions of the original Revelation.

Moshe, hearing the voice of the Shechinah resonating through his own throat, is the best example of the 'I-I' relationship. He is one with the Divine 'I' and yet he retains his individuality, as evidenced by his use of the recurring term "me" throughout *Devarim*. He transcends himself and yet simultaneously includes himself, which is a sign of *Atzmus* / Essence-consciousness. We read the Book of Devarim in Av because Av is calling us to this Essential state of 'inclusive transcendence', which is a necessary ingredient in cultivating the levels of 'deep listening' so needed in these difficult times.

Our Sages elaborate on the destruction of the Second Beis ha-Mikdash and the hardships that then befell the People of Israel, in the Talmud, Tractate *Gittin* / The Laws of Divorce. Nothing is by mere coincidence, as Reb Tzadok of Lublin teaches, and certainly not something so essential as the tractate of Talmud wherein the above events are recorded and reflected upon. The fact that the destruction and exile of the people is detailed in Gittin shows us that the entire narrative of the destruction and exile from our homeland is a form of *Gittin*, a type of 'divorce' or separation between Hashem and Klal Yisrael (however external and temporary it may be).

Non-Separation in Separation

The very opening of Tractate Gittin deals with the details and requirements of a *Get* / bill of divorce. There are 12 lines in the manuscript of a Get, says *Tosefos* (*Gittin*, 2a), because the numerical value of the word *Get* is 12. But then Tosefos adds, in the name of the Geonim (R. Hai and Saadia Gaon), that the reason there are 12 lines in the document is because the Torah calls a Get, a "book that separates", and the primary book or *Sefer* is the actual Torah. In the Torah, what "separates" one book from the other are four empty lines. Between the first and second books of the Torah (*Bereishis* and *Shemos*) there are four lines, between the second and third books there are another four lines, and between the third and fourth books another four lines — adding up to 12 empty lines in total. The empty space between the books, the separation between the books is like a Get, and thus an actual Get needs 12 lines.

However, there is also a fifth book, the book of Devarim, and between the fourth and fifth book there are another four empty lines. According to Tosefos, this 'separation' between the fourth and fifth book is not counted as a real 'separation' since the fifth book is basically a 'repetition' of, or a 'return' to, what is in the first four books; this keeps the total of 'dividing lines' in the Torah to 12, the number of lines in a Get.

Inwardly, this means that with any separation where there is an eventual 'returning' or 'repeating', there is in effect no real separation. The fifth book is thus not part of the *Get Kerisus* / document (or concept) of severance represented by the first four books. This non-separative separation is more like a pause, a moment of 'taking space', so to speak. It is like a movement of inhaling, or of pulling back and crouching down, to jump higher into unity; a temporary retreat in order to reconnect with renewed strength and permanence.

This is the story of our exile; it is only a pause, a drawing back. The *Churban* / destruction and exile from the Land of Israel is meant only to create within us a desire to reunite with Hashem in a unity that is greater than ever before. It is like the two dimensions of Av, represented by the two 'holidays' Tisha b'Av and Tu b'Av, respectively. The purpose of the 'separation' in the first half of Av is only to bring about a higher, deeper *Yichud* / unification in the second half. Therefore, the Churban and exile cannot be considered a 'Get', *Chas veShalom* / Heaven forbid. Similarly, the 'rebuke' of Moshe which we read in Devarim, speaking of a harsh separation and exile, is not a Get. Rather, it is a temporary drawing back so that we can launch into full actualization of connection and ultimately, Redemption.

There is a fascinating Medrash that clearly supports this idea (*Yalkut*, Yirmiyahu, in the beginning): "The Lion (i.e., Nevuchadnetzar. *Yirmiyahu*, 4:7) arose in the month of the lion (Leo) and destroyed *Ariel* / the Lion of G-d, (an epithet of Jerusalem in *Yeshayahu*, 29:1)…*Al Menas* / on the condition that the Lion (Hashem) will return in the month of the lion (Leo) and rebuild Ariel (Jerusalem)". *Al Menas* is a concept in Halacha. When one does something "on condition", such as knocking down a home *Al Menas* that he will build another one in its place, then the act of destroying actually becomes an act of building; it is no longer considered a destructive act. In this way,

Hashem allows for the destruction of the Beis haMikdash and the eventual exile. These were *Al Menas* the rebuilding of the Third and permanent Holy Temple, and the ultimate and final Redemption (*Chidushim U'biurim*, Hilchos Beis HaBechirah, Sicha 11). This is also the reason we begin reading the fifth book of Devarim in Av. The harshness and 'separation' expressed in the rebukes are *Al Menas* / on the condition that we manifest a higher, deeper level of unity — ultimately catalyzing the birth of Moshiach Consciousness.

In this way, the destruction of the Temples that occurs on Tisha b'Av, representing the end of the old *Yesh* / paradigmatic existence, is *Al Menas* so that there should be an existential *Ayin* / void or empty state that allows for the birth of a new Yesh, i.e., Moshiach. Only the 'death' of the old allows for the emergence of the new. This initial destruction opens the possibility for the eventual building of the Third and Permanent Beis haMikdash, which will usher in a time of *Geula Sheleima* / complete and final Redemption and the revealing of the Ultimate Oneness of Hashem.

The structure of the created world (post Tzimtzum) is that there is "evening and then there is morning, day one"; the way of the world is that darkness comes before light (*Shabbos*, 77b). Since the teleology of history is directed toward the universal illumination of Moshiach, when the world of *Yichud* / unity and revealing of Hashem's presence will be manifest for all to see, everything that occurs up until that point in history can be compared to a long, dark 'night' leading to a bright, new 'day'. Thus, we learn that: every fall is for the purpose of a higher rise; every breaking is for the purpose of a deeper healing; every destruction is for the purpose of a more creative construction; and every death is for the purpose of refining life. Darkness, death, falling, breaking, exile, sin, destruction — these are not ends unto themselves and have no real existence, as the only true existence is Hashem and the revealed Yichud.

At present, *Galus* / exile brings forth and gives birth to the future *Geulah* / Redemption. Appropriately, the Tur points out that Tisha b'Av falls out on the same day (of the week) as the first day of Pesach: the Exodus from Egypt (*Orach Chayim*, 428, from Medrash Eichah Rabba, Pesichta, 18. See also *Ramah*, Orach Chayim, 476:2). This implies that there is an associative resonance between these two days, no matter how different they appear on the surface. This reveals that there is a *Bechina* / an essential point within Tishah b'Av that, although very painful and traumatic, is also a form of 'Redemption'. The destruction of the Temples signaled the end of a time in history wherein the Temple could simultaneously coexist with the presence of idol worship, or even internal strife and division within the Jewish people. The closing of the old cycle ushered in the possibility for the Third Beis haMikdash, which will bring about total Redemption and the elimination of all evil, death, exile, destruction, night, sin and strife forever. The Third Temple will initiate a time and space of total immersion into the world of *Yichud* / unity, speedily in our days.

SEASON OF THE YEAR

HE HEAT OF THE SUMMER CAN SEEM 'HOSTILE' OR DESTRUCTIVE, and thus in Biblical Hebrew, heat is occasionally referred to as *Chorev*, which is related to the word *Churban* / destruction. As we have explored, the physical heat that characterizes the beginning of Av mirrors the historical events of intense spiritual destruction that occurred at the beginning of Av. The first nine days of Av are days of mourning the destruction of Jerusalem and the First and Second Holy Temples, culminating with the ninth day, Tisha b'Av. However, on the heels of this day of destruction comes the 15th day, Tu b'Av, a day of great joy and love. This is also when there is at least a subtle shift in climate. The heat is mitigated and balanced, bringing a breath of relief — both physically and spiritually.*

"There were no greater days of joy than *Tu b'Av* / the 15th of Av and Yom Kippur…. On these days the daughters of Jerusalem used to go out in white garments which they borrowed in order not to shame anyone who didn't have their own. The daughters of Jerusalem came out and danced in the vineyards, exclaiming, 'Young man, lift up your eyes and see, what you choose for yourself'" (Mishnah, *Ta'anis*, 4:8). The wailing for the 'death' of the Temple on the Ninth of Av suddenly gives way to the singing and dancing

---

* Once Av enters, we should diminish in matters of joy. And if a person has a court case in Av, they should try to push it off. *Ta'anis*, 29b. *Shulchan Aruch*, Orach Chayim, 551:1. There are those who argue that Tu b'Av is merely a break from the general mourning of Av, and the cautionary statements above therefore apply to the entire month of Av. *Magen Avraham*, Orach Chayim 551:2, *Mishnah Berurah*, 551:1 and *Piskei Teshuvah* ad loc. See also; Yerushalmi, *Ta'anis* 4:6. However, the Chasam Sofer writes that Tu b'Av marks the end of the mourning period. As such, there are those who argue that the above ruling concerning the decreasing of joy and pushing off of court dates would only apply during the first part of Av. *Nemukei Orach Chayim*, 551:1; *Korban Nisanel*, Ta'anis 4:5. Indeed, there is already a lessening of negativity from the Tenth of Av forward. It seems clear from the Zohar that the 'negativity' of this month is only for the first nine days, and not the entire month. *Zohar* 2, Yisro, 78b. The Magid of Koznitz teaches (*Avodas Yisrael*, Devarim) that there is a Yichud of the Name *Ado-nai* present in the world from the Tenth of Av until Sukkos, as hinted at in the following calculations: The Name *Ado-nai* is comprised of four letters: Aleph/1, Dalet/4, Nun/50 and Yud/10. The Nun/50 corresponds to the 50 days from the Tenth of Av until the end of Elul. The Yud/10 corresponds to the 'Ten Days of Teshuvah' between (and including) Rosh Hashanah and Yom Kippur. The Dalet/4 corresponds to the 4 days between Yom Kippur and Sukkos. The Aleph/1 corresponds to the first day of Sukkos.

of rebirth on the Fifteenth, with a marked focus on the future, as evidenced by the day's emphasis on finding one's soul-mate and getting married. Great mourning thus gives way to great joy during the month of Av.

ᘐᖇ

THE HOLIDAY OF THE MONTH:
Tisha b'Av

EMBRACING PAIN

O N PESACH, WE RECLINE ON PLUSH CHAIRS LIKE KINGS
and queens as we triumphantly recount the story of our
Exodus and Redemption from slavery. On Tisha b'Av,
in stark contrast, we sit on the floor as mourners and tearfully recite
Eicha / Lamentations and Kinus / mournful poetic texts recounting
the tragedies of our people's dispersals and destructions throughout
the ages. On both days, we are encouraged to feel these historical
events as if we were experiencing them in the present moment; the
choreographed posturing and bodily positioning for these exercises
in animated memory are cues to help us connect to the spirit of the
day. From this more experiential and existential perspective, it can

be understood that Tisha b'Av is not only a day that we mourn the destructions of the Temples and several other historical calamities that occurred on this day in the past. It is also called a *Bechiy l'Doros* / a day set aside for weeping throughout the generations (*Ta'anis,* 29a). This means that Tisha b'Av is a day on which we are meant to grieve, lament, and really experience *Aveilus* / mourning for all of the *current* pain and hardship in our lives and in the world. Tisha b'Av encourages us to embrace all of the overwhelming sadness, pain and unredeemed, unperfected realities in the world.

Intense and powerful emotions such as pain, sadness, and vulnerability, even to the point of tears, are very real and should not be completely repressed or utterly avoided. Indeed, to be truly human we need to embrace every emotion, albeit within a healthy, supportive and productive context. Tisha b'Av is the time to let our guard down and embrace these dark, heavy and often cathartic emotions. *

Each day of our lives contains aspects and energies rooted within the various holidays of the year. Some moments in the day are similar to Pesach, where we feel physically, emotionally, mentally and spiritually liberated; some moments during the day feel more introspective, like Yom Kippur. There are times within a day when we feel overjoyed like on Purim, and there are times we feel sad like on Tisha b'Av. This is because the *Partzuf haZemanim* / the structure (or personality) of the seasons is represented within the

---

* Aaron passed away in Av, and once he passed away, the 'Clouds of Glory' that protected Klal Yisrael were gone (*Ta'anis,* 9a). Thus Av, certainly the first part of Av, is a time when we feel more spiritually exposed and vulnerable.

Partzuf haYamim / the structure (or personality) of days. In the *Partzuf haZemanim*, the holidays of the year occur once a year, representing the fullest embodiment of their respective qualities. From the *Partzuf haZemanim*, all of those qualities, emotions and energies flow into the individual days of the year, represented by the *Partzuf haYamim*.

From the perspective of the *Partzuf haZemanim*, all the joy of the year is concentrated into the days of Sukkos, and all the atonement of the year is concentrated into Yom Kippur. We then draw from Sukkos all the joy that will enliven each day of the year, and we draw from Yom Kippur all the atonement manifest within each day of the year. Thus, every day becomes an open vessel receiving and circulating an energetic infusion from each of the holy-days of the year.

Just as there is a *Moed* / holiday or appointed time to encounter the Divine through happiness (Sukkot) or liberation (Pesach), there is a Moed for encountering the Divine through *Bechiya* / weeping, sadness, and pain (Tisha b'Av). This day is designed and dedicated to cultivating and containing all the sadness of the year.

Tisha b'Av is referred to as a *Moed* / holiday: "קרא עלי מועד לשבר לשבר בחורי / He has called a Moed / against me to crush my young men" (*Eicha*, 1:15). This passage does not refer to Tisha b'Av as a Moed merely because of the hidden, positive energy of the day, for as we know, Moshiach is born on this day; nor is this meant to imply that there is a reason to celebrate, because it could have been even worse, as the Divine wrath was primarily released on 'wood and stones' rather than upon the people themselves (Chasam Sofer, *Toras Moshe*, Ma'asei,

p. 738). Rather, Tisha b'Av is actually a Moed of hardship. It is a holiday focused on destruction, loss and pain.

Today, exile still permeates the world. There is deep pain and hardship almost everywhere, often hidden beneath a facade of superficial joy. On almost every day of the year, we need to actively ensure that joy and positivity lift us out of the pain and sadness we feel for our own physical, mental, emotional or spiritual predicaments — as well as the pain of other people and the planet itself. However, on Tisha b'Av we take the time to honestly acknowledge and embrace the state of *Galus* / exile that we live in, including all its pain and vulnerability.

In fact, it is often precisely within peak moments of great joy or perilous moments of great sadness that we most viscerally sense the Hand of Hashem in our lives. In other words, we are able to more easily feel Hashem's power and presence in the revealed miracles of life, as well as, paradoxically, in their opposite. This is the deeper reason why Tisha b'Av, the 22nd day from the 17th of Tamuz, parallels the holiday of Shemini Atzeres, the 22nd day of Tishrei (See *Maharsha*, Bechoros, 8a). Unlike the previous seven days of Sukkos, where offerings were brought by the Jews on behalf of all the nations of the world, on Shemini Atzeres Hashem says, 'I want to be alone with you for one more day' (*Yalkut Shimoni*, Pinchas, 782). This private, intimate holiday is likened to a "small banquet made by the King for His beloved" (Bamidbar, *Rashi* 28: 35). This sensation of being 'alone with the King', of being called into the Presence of Hashem, is acutely felt both in times of elation and closeness, such as on Shemini Atzeres, as well as in times of great anxiety and alienation, such as on Tisha b'Av. On Tisha b'Av, we acknowledge and embrace the exile that we live in, with all its pain and vulner-ability; specifically from that place, we sense the presence and the Hand of the Creator within these very hardships.

Unlike all the other fast days of the year, Tisha b'Av is not a time for *Tachanunim* — meaning that we do not recite *Tachanun* / supplications or *Selichos* / words that stimulate Divine forgiveness. Rather, we are encouraged simply to open ourselves up to experi-ence a state of mourning and *Bechiya* / weeping.

The word *Bechiyah* comes from the word *Nevuchim* / confused, lost, with a lack of options, as in the verse, *Nevuchim Hem Bamid-bar* / wandering in confusion, (hemmed in by) the Desert (*Shemos*, 14:3). The feeling of Nevuchim is that you are stuck; you cannot go forward, but neither can you go back to where you once were.

We cry when we are overwhelmed by a situation that seems out of our control and beyond our proven methods of coping. When we are at a loss and when the mind cannot grasp what is happen-ing, it seems like there is nothing to do, and there is indeed nothing that can be done. The only thing we can do is cry. This is the way the mind and body release the tension of overwhelming immobi-lization.

Another word for 'tears' is *Dimah*. *Dimah* is related to the word *Dema*, which means 'mixed' or entangled (*Kesav V'hakbalah*, Shemos, 22:38). We weep when we are mixed up, not sure where to turn or entangled in a web of cognitive dissonance. Paradoxically, the tears themselves can make our vision even more blurry. Even when tears are ultimately clarifying, both our physical and mental vision can become temporarily obscured in the process. In the midst of our sadness, we may even feel we are living in a world of *Tohu* / chaos and confusion.

On Tisha b'Av we are meant to sit with these states, without trying to avoid them. Sometimes we need to feel the full weight of the Churban and the collective conditions of exile, confusion and dissonance throughout the world. We need to feel an acute sense of mourning in order to access the immediate sense of destruction that permeates our history as well as the world in general. Commemorating these historical and external calamities is also meant to bring us into intimate contact with the inner brokenness present within each of our own lives and the lives of our loved ones. In the words of the Rambam: "There are days when the entire Jewish people fast because of the calamities that occurred to them in order to arouse [their] hearts and initiate [them in] the paths of *Teshuvah*. This serves as a reminder of *our* negative conduct and that of our ancestors...which brought these calamities upon them and upon *us*. In remembering these things we return to goodness...." (*Hilchos Ta'anis*, 5:1).

On Tisha b'Av, even learning Torah is not allowed. The reason for this, according to one perspective, is that learning Torah brings joy (*Ta'anis*, 30a, *Rashi* ad loc), which is prohibited on this day. From a slightly different perspective, we should not take our mind off the *Churban* for even one moment during this day (*Maharsha*, Ta'anis 30a). In both cases, during the entire 24 hours of Tisha b'Av we should try to be in a state of *Aveilus* / mourning and remembering: the destructions of the Temples; the resultant and recurring exiles into the diaspora that we are still presently suffering from; and also all the destructions and chaos in our own lives, which are also a result of the same, 'original' exile.

Other halachic guidelines for remaining in *Aveilus* on Tisha b'Av include: sitting on the floor instead of on regular chairs; refraining from bathing; refraining from wearing leather shoes; refraining from intimate relations; and even refraining from socializing.

The experience of *Aveilus* is very similar to the experience of a *Menudah* / an outcast or person who was temporarily excommunicated due to certain crimes. A mourner can feel very alone, separated from others, as if no one understands what they are going through. They may feel generally cut off, as if excommunicated from the Source of All Life. For a person in deep mourning, there is a deafening silence (*Moed Katan*, 15a).

€

HASHEM IS PRESENT EVEN WITHIN OUR CHESER

On a deeper level, sitting on the floor, refraining from bathing and descending into silence are all gestures which affirm that Hashem is with us even here; even within our condition of being 'down and dirty' and 'on the floor', and even when we find ourselves at the lowest level completely immersed in pain, Hashem is with us. Hashem is with us even in our disheveled state, in our inability to speak, in our incompleteness and in our Cheser. In fact, it also works the other way around. In one Medrashic image (*Eichah Rabba*, 1:1), seeing the destruction of the Beis haMikdash, Hashem asks, "What do earthly kings do in this situation? They dim the lights. I will do the same." and Hashem turned off the Heavenly lights. "What else do they do? They turn over their beds…they take off their shoes…sit on the floor in silence…they cry… I will do the same." says Hashem. The Shechinah, so to speak, sits on the floor, and we too, who are sympathetic to the plight of the Shechinah, also sit on the floor in solidarity.

The point is that Tisha b'Av is all about inhabiting and engaging the place of *Cheser* / lack. As we mentioned, Tisha b'Av is connected to the Cheser or 'absence' symbolized by the *Gid haNasheh*, that which is 'removed' from Yaakov, rendering him incomplete (and by association, ourselves as well). On Tisha b'Av we work to embrace the Cheser, the void in our lives, and the things we need that are 'missing'. We embrace the *Churbanos* / destructions of both Temples, as well as those in our own personal lives. When we do so, we can discover that Hashem is present in destruction just as in creation, in tears just as in joy, in the unclean just as in the clean and in the ugly just as in the beautiful. Hashem is present even in the death of a loved one, in hardships, in relationship problems, in fear and in anxiety — Hashem is always there with you, no matter where *there* is.

Our Sages tell us: "Why were the Sages of old, those who wrote the Amidah prayer, called 'Men of the Great Assembly'? For they

restored the crown of the Divine Attributes to its ancient completeness. [For] Moshe had come and said: 'The great G-d, the
mighty and the awesome' (*Devarim* 10:17). Then Yirmiyahu came
and said: 'Foreigners are destroying the Temple. Where are, then,
Hashem's awesome deeds?' So he omitted [the attribute] 'the awesome'. Daniel came and said: 'Foreigners are enslaving His sons.
Where are Hashem's mighty deeds?' He therefore omitted the
word 'mighty'. But they, the Men of the Great Assembly, came and
said: 'On the contrary! (See *Nechemya* 9)…Therein lie His awesome
powers: For but for the fear of Him, how could one [single] nation
persist among the [many] nations!'" (*Yuma*, 69b). Indeed, sometimes
we feel the awesome power of Hashem precisely within our per-
severance despite our hardships and suffering, in our unbreakable
connection despite our sadness and pain.

It is taught that there is no sadness in the Presence of Hashem
— at least in regard to the 'outer chambers', (meaning: 'in the way
that we *connect* with Hashem'). However, on Tisha b'Av, because of
the Churban, Hashem is sad, so-to-speak, even in the 'outer chambers' (*Chagigah*, 5b). This means that on Tisha b'Av we can connect
with Hashem even within our separation and sadness. This day
then gives us the strength to connect with Hashem throughout the
year whenever we are going through some form of personal 'Tisha
b'Av', so to speak. In other words, on the day of Tisha b'Av we are
given the *Moed* / time or point of encounter, to realize Hashem is
present everywhere: in every situation, even in our sadness, loss,
disconnection and deficiency.

There is something quite puzzling about the day(s) of the week
when the first and second Beis haMikdash were destroyed. We

know that the second Beis haMikdash began to be destroyed on Motzei Shabbos, right after Shabbos (*Ta'anis.* 29a, *Erchin*, 11b); moreover, the second Beis haMikdash was destroyed on Shabbos itself (according to the Yerushalmi [*Ta'anis*, 4:5], it was destroyed on Rosh Chodesh, and we know that the 9th of Av that year was on Sunday). From all days of the week we would think that Shabbos itself would be the least appropriate day for such destruction, as Shabbos is beyond the world of destruction (*Shem M'Shemuel*, Vayakhel), and furthermore, that the special quality of Shabbos would perhaps even protect the Beis ha-Mikdash. And yet it is specifically so that we would be able to seek out and find Hashem's presence, the light of the Shechinah, even and especially within our exile, that the Temples were destroyed on or right after Shabbos (*Yearos Devash*, 1, Derush 13).

Shabbos in time is like the Beis haMikdash in space (*Pri Tzadik*, Vayakhel). The Shechinah rested within the Beis haMikdash in space, and similarly rests within the dimensions of time on Shabbos. When the Beis haMikdash was destroyed, the (revealed presence of the) Shechinah departed on the level of space, and yet because it was Shabbos, the Shechinah remained enclothed within, and accessible through, time. And so, as we physically went into exile, the Shechinah has come with us as we traveled through time. From the day of the Churban forwards, and especially on Tisha b'Av itself, we have a Moed, a time set aside, where we can and should deeply feel Hashem's absence; at the same time, we must also realize Hashem's presence everywhere, and in every situation: even in our exile, alienation, deficiencies and sadness.

On Tisha b'Av, we are elevated to the level of Rabbi Akiva who was able to proclaim *Hashem Echad* / Hashem is One, even while being tortured and killed by the Romans in a most horrific manner (*Berachos*, 61b). He was thus able to recognize and connect with the presence of the Compassionate One even in the most extreme difficulty.

Our Sages tell us (*Chagigah*, 14b; *Zohar* I, 26b; *Tikunei Zohar*, Tikun 40) that there were four Sages who entered the *Pardes* / Orchard of Paradise by utilizing Divine Names (*Rashi, Tosefos*, ad loc). These four were Ben Azzai, Ben Zoma, Acher (Elisha ben Abuyah) and Rabbi Akiva. Rabbi Akiva instructed them prior to their ascension: "When you come to the place of pure marble stones, do not say, 'Water, water!'" The Talmud continues: "Ben Azzai gazed and died. Ben Zoma gazed and lost his sanity. Acher cut down the plantings (i.e., became a heretic). Rabbi Akiva entered and exited in peace" (Bavli 14b says Rabbi Akiva *exited* in peace, or ascended in peace and descended in peace (ibid, 15b). However, the Yerushalmi in *Chagigah* 2:1 says he entered and exited in peace).

'Water' is a symbol for desire. Rabbi Akiva warned the other Sages and instructed them: 'when you enter into the mystical experience, no matter how you perceive this inner reality, never say there are two *waters*. Do not make the mistake of thinking that there is a higher, nobler, Divine desire and a separate, lower human desire, which is lust and depravity. There is only One Reality: *Hashem Echad*. Ultimately, all desire is Hashem's desire.'

When Elisha ben Abuyah entered the mystical orchard and beheld the Angel Metatron sitting down on a throne, he became a heretic. His heresy sprang from his belief, based on this vision, that there are two forces, rather than one, active in the universe

— a positive, Divine force of light, goodness, creation and beauty, and a second force of darkness, negativity, destruction and ugliness (*Rabbeinu Chananel* on Chagigah, 14b. Rabbi Hai Gaon quoted in *haK'tov*, Eyn Yaakov, Chagigah 14b # 11).

Previously, when the mother of young Elisha realized the beauty and majesty of the Torah, she desired that her son become a Torah scholar. She therefore encouraged him in this regard. As he grew older, he too became enchanted by the beauty and majesty of Torah. However, Elisha was also drawn to the beauty of Greek culture and arts, and his tongue never tired of singing Greek melodies (Yerushalmi, *Megillah* 1:9). Based on his understanding, he felt that Hashem's presence could be found within the beauty and harmony of life, but not in the ugliness or hardship. This was ultimately Elisha's mistake; he could not comprehend that Hashem's Presence and Oneness extended into and even embraced and enveloped darkness and suffering. He thereby limited the Infinite Oneness of Hashem, and conceived of a dualistic, conflicted universe.

Elisha thought that the Divine image ought to be 'standing' rather than 'sitting'; Hashem must only be upright, majestic, beautiful, bright and powerful. When he entered the mystical Orchard and saw the Divine image 'sitting', he thought that this must not be of Hashem, and therefore that it must be an image of some other power or entity. He concluded that there must be two forces: one 'standing' image representing beauty, majesty and power, and one 'sitting' image representing lowness, darkness, ugliness and lack. He did not see Hashem's Unified Presence permeating the apparent opposites of light and darkness, beauty and ugliness, creation and destruction; rather, he sensed two-ness, and said, in effect, "water-water". At this point, Elisha's name became *Acher* / Other, as he had identified with a belief in 'otherness' — namely, that there is Hashem and something other than Hashem. Having alienated himself from the truth of Oneness within the 'inner chamber' of the Orchard, he became a heretic.

Another teaching reverses these connotations of the 'inner and outer chambers'. The Book of Tehilim says, *Yashes Choshech Sisro* / He made darkness His secret place (*Tehilim*, 18:12). Our Sages ask if there can indeed be 'darkness' within the intimate Presence of Hashem. They respond: "In the inner chambers there is only Light, but in the outer chambers there is darkness" (*Chagigah*, 12b). From the perspective of the 'outer chamber' — from our constricted, limited vantage point — it does appear that there is darkness in the world: a Churban and a Galus. However, we can also conceive that "He *made* darkness." It is the Creator Himself behind the appearance of darkness; the One True Existence is within darkness as well as light.

On Tisha b'Av, we embrace our fears, darkness, ugliness and Cheser. In this painful embrace, we must strive to recognize that Hashem is present even there. Even though on this day we should certainly sensitize ourselves to the feeling of being an *Avel* / mourner, or one who is dejected and lost, without a home or center of gravity, this contemplation and identification must be understood as temporary. The truth is that, even though we do not yet have a revealed Temple, the Divine Presence never actually left. The Omnipresent One is with us wherever we go, inwardly and outwardly.

☾

FINDING HASHEM
WITHIN DARKNESS

Most people are actually conditioned to recognize Hashem's Presence as a result of difficult or tragic experiences more so than through experiences of light and happiness. This is because we tend to turn outwards in times of joy and turn inwards in times of tragedy. Anguish tends to bring people into spiritual introspection and self-evaluation. Moreover, pain can rapidly break down our egoic resistance to the experience of the Transcendent, opening us up to connect specifically from within our constriction.

Without denying the devastating tragedies of Tisha b'Av, there was also a redeeming factor; the people who lived through these events were shocked out of their spiritual complacency. They were shaken to their core and had no recourse but to return to the depths of their true selves. This is the ultimately positive import of those events, and this is why Tisha b'Av is considered a holiday, a *Moed* / special time conducive to Divine encounter.

Unlike other holidays, of course, this one is 'celebrated', or observed, by fasting and mourning. In order to tap into the day's positive purpose — to shake ourselves out of our own complacency — we must tap into our brokenness. Activities such as fasting and reciting lamentations sensitize us not only to the tragedy of the historical exiles, but to our own inner exile and existential separation from who we really are. We, too, can allow Tisha b'Av to motivate us to truly transform.

Our Sages point out that, "Our vision comes not from the white of the eye, rather from the black (pupil)" (*Medrash Rabbah*, Vayikra 31:8). While this is literally true, there is also a deeper message imparted in this teaching. Darkness, ugliness, sadness and difficulty often allow us to see more clearly than when life is light, beautiful, joyous and easy. Just as vision registers by means of contrast, the light of life is perceived by means of contrast with its seeming opposite.

Sometimes clarity — about our life, who we are and what we are meant to be doing — comes specifically in moments when we are faced with intense hardship. Our priorities and needs become sharper and more immediate. We look with more honesty at our lives when our sense of contentment is suspended.

After we have very viscerally suspended our sense of contentment on Tisha b'Av and celebrated Hashem's presence in Cheser and absence, we can then be open to the revelation of *Tu b'Av* / the 15th of Av just a few days later. When the moon of Av becomes full, the wrathful ugliness of Tisha b'Av becomes revealed as love, purity and beauty.

☾

FROM TISHA B'AV TO TU B'AV

On Tu b'Av, under the light of the full moon, the unmarried women of Israel would go out into the fields in plain, white garments. Our Sages teach, 'The beautiful ones — and they were all in essence beautiful (*Nedarim*, 66a) — would call to the young men: *behold our beauty, lift up your eyes to see beauty* (*Ta'anis*, 31a)!'

Our Sages tell us: "There were no greater days of joy than Tu b'Av and Yom Kippur... On these days the daughters of Jerusalem would go out in white garments, which each had borrowed in order not to shame anyone who had none. They danced in the vineyards, exclaiming, 'Young man, lift up your eyes and see what you choose for yourself'" (Mishnah, *Ta'anis* 4:8).

On Tisha b'Av, following the episode of the Meraglim, it had been decreed upon those who were redeemed from Egypt that they would not enter the Promised Land. Rather, it would be their off-spring born in the Desert who would enter the Land, while they themselves would die in the Desert. On Tu b'Av, this dying of the older generation ceased, and therefore it was and is a time impreg-nated with the hope of a renewed future.

On Tu b'Av, we are reborn from the ruins of Tisha b'Av. Even after Hashem's 'home' has been destroyed, we suddenly turn our focus to building and moving forward. Unmarried people are en-couraged to find their soulmate and build their home, even amidst the rubble. Mourning thus spontaneously gives way to great joy. What is the cause and meaning of this radical shift in conscious-ness?

In the calendar, just as in life, there are ups and there are downs. Although the ups — the light, joy, redemption — seem to be polar opposites of the lows — the darkness, sadness and mourning — all are in fact expressions of the Infinite One. Experientially, it is often from within darkness that the highest light emerges. This is because the light that resides within the depths of darkness is so intense that it cannot be perceived under normal circumstances. This is why the night seems to be darkest just before the moment of daybreak. On Tu b'Av, when the moon is full, there is a bursting forth of the light hidden within the tragedies of Tisha b'Av.

This dynamic, which sounds counterintuitive, is actually found within the most material laws of physics: the lower you crouch the higher you can jump. When you pull strongly in one direction, the release in the opposite direction is more intense. In our context, the deeper the level of darkness, separation and concealment, the greater the longing and yearning to connect, unite and reveal. Tisha b'Av is the deepest point of darkness, the nadir of *Cheser* and longing. The product of this longing is manifest on the day of Tu b'Av. This is similar to a theme we explored earlier: the concealed 'good' of Day Two of Creation, the day of separation between the upper and lower waters, is only revealed on Day Three. On Day Three there is a unification of the waters. Similarly, the 'good' of Tisha b'Av is only revealed as 'good' when Tu b'Av arrives — the day when 'good' and 'bad' are revealed as ultimately one.

It is known that the Nine Days of Av correspond to the nine days of Sukkos (as counted in the Diaspora, where two days of Chag are celebrated instead of one, bringing the count of days in Sukkos to nine, rather than eight). According to this correspondence, Tisha b'Av parallels Simchas Torah — one of the most ecstatically joyful days of the year (*Darchei Chayim v'Shalom*, p. 224-225).* Although these two days appear to be opposites, one necessarily leads to the other.

---

* Alternatively, according to the original eight days of Sukkos as practiced in the Land of Israel, Tisha b'Av parallels Shemini Atzeres, as the '22nd day' from 17th

On a deeper level, selfless grief is inseparable from selfless joy.

On Simchas Torah, we recite verses that express the triumphant joy of Redemption and the coming Days of Moshiach. Our Sages tell us that Moshiach was, or 'is', born on Tisha b'Av. When the Temple was destroyed, the old light was extinguished so that the new, greater Light of Moshiach could be revealed (Maharal, *Netzach Yisrael* 27:10). Such brilliant Light can only be revealed from within deep darkness. As mentioned previously, there has to be a total *Bit-ul* / nullification of the previous *Tzurah* / form in order for a new form to emerge. The unifying Light of Moshiach Consciousness can only be born within the all-consuming yearning and alienation of Tisha b'Av. This dynamic is part of the very fabric of Creation, and reveals much about who we are and how we function as human beings.

☾

of Tamuz would be aligned with the 22nd day of Tishrei (*Maharsha*, Bechoros, 8a). According to some, Tisha b'Av also parallels the night of our Exodus from Egypt (See *Tur*, Orach Chayim, 428. *Medrash Eichah Rabba*, Pesichta, 18).

THE DYNAMICS OF REVEALING
LIGHT WITHIN DARKNESS

To reiterate: the experience of separation inevitably creates longing, which then brings about a deeper and higher level of unity; this process is woven into the very fabric of Creation, including within our own human psychology and emotional patterns.

We can see this dynamic illustrated in the deeper narrative of Creation, as revealed by the Arizal. Creation occurs through a process of *Tzimtzum* / constriction and withdrawal of the Infinite Light of the Creator, which follows Hashem's initial desire to create an 'other' with whom to share, love and connect with. This withdrawal in effect leaves room for finitude to be revealed; for only once the Infinite Light is limited or put aside, so to speak, can the world as we know it begin to emerge. This Tzimtzum creates a vacated space or fertile void within which newly created beings may exist, as well as long for reconnection with the Infinite Light of Unity 'beyond' Tzimtzum. In other words, the ultimate purpose of the withdrawal of the Infinite Light and the appearance of both physical and existential separation is to create spiritual longing; and the purpose of this longing is to then catalyze the subsequent revelation of a Higher Unity. This is specifically not the revelation of a unity that would erase the state of longing, which is, on some level, essential for perpetual growth and striving. The point is to discover the deeper Unity *within* the state of longing. This discovery reveals the Unity that is ever-present, even amidst separation.

Following the Tzimtzum there is a *Chalal* / vacuum or empty space. Within this void, a *Kav* / thin ray of light beams into the Chalal. The Kav is a focused 'line' of light that is still connected to the Infinite Light beyond and 'above' the state of Tzimtzum. The word *Kav* is also related to another Hebrew word that means 'hope' (T**ikv**ah) — further hinting at an experience of yearning, aspiration and a deep desire to reconnect with the Source of the Kav, the Infinite Light.

Yet, from the perspective of the Chalal, which is the place of our human existence, characterized as it is by emptiness and separation, there will always be longing. In other words: there will always be a necessary sense of lack and a corresponding drive toward fulfilment. From this (our) perspective, the Tzimtzum is real. The bridge separating the Infinite and the finite is uncrossable, and *Cheser* / lack is part and parcel of Creation. Due to these dynamics of Creation, the way to reconnect to the reality 'beyond' Tzimtzum is to deeply desire and yearn for it; this longing is itself the bridge over the abyss of our isolation.

In this 'post-Tzimtzum' world of ours, you may think that if you get what you desire, your desire will be quenched. The truth is, the above-mentioned desire will never be fully satisfied. There is a place within us that is truly post-Tzimtzum — is a place of unquenchable incompleteness. However, there is a purpose in this existential incompleteness; and that is to create a desire to reconnect with the place of completeness, which is the unity *prior* to Tzimtzum.

The part of us that is post-Tzimtzum — where Cheser / lack, longing and separation are apparently absolute — is termed *Nefesh*.

This is the place within us where we experience, cultivate and channel such movement, fluctuation, effort and longing. This level of being is referred to as the world of *Pirud* / separation. The part of us that is pre-Tzimtzum, beyond separation and in changeless unity, is called *Yechidah* / unified. This is our effortless essence beyond movement and separation. From the perspective of Yechidah there is only Unity; no desire or yearning, no 'outside' or separate 'past', and thus there is no exile, destruction or Tzimtzum (See R. Hillel of Paritch, *Pelach HaRimon*, Shemos, p. 7). In Yechidah-consciousness, Moshiach is 'already here', as there is no 'there' and in fact no 'future', as all potential is manifest in the present and eternal now.

Both of these perspectives, the pre- and post-Tzimtzum dimensions within us, are 'real' in our experience of life. Pain, hardship, exile, destruction, death and separation are certainly all real. And from this perspective, we long, we wait, we yearn and we work for redemption, life and unity. At the same time, a part of us knows that there is no separation, no exile, no destruction and no death. From this perspective, reality is always perfect, whole, 'redeemed' and unified.

Practically, this means that we need to acknowledge and embrace our pain and suffering, properly mourn our individual and collective losses and yearn for a better world. This is the practice of Tisha b'Av. At the same time, we also need to have faith that life is always perfect exactly as it is. We hope and pray and yearn that the Yechidah reality will become revealed in this world of apparently fragmented time and space, and that we will see the *Geulah Sheleimah* / Complete Redemption here and now.

☾

THE UNITY REVEALED
WITHIN YEARNING:

Our Sages rule that it is appropriate for a husband and wife to have relations immediately before he leaves town on a business trip. Within the inner dimensions of this halachah there is an acknowledgment that passion is most intense between lovers when they are about to part ways, and thus it is the most opportune time for intimacy. Similarly, at the time of the destruction of Jerusalem and the beginning of separation and exile from Hashem, we find the greatest intimacy between the Divine Lover and His beloved People.

When the People of Israel were not aligned with the Creator, the two golden *Keruvim* / Cherubim that adorned the Ark of the Covenant miraculously turned and faced away from each other. When Israel was aligned with Hashem, the Keruvim turned to face each other (*Baba Basra*, 99b). Yet, at the moment when the Temple was destroyed and we were driven into exile, the Keruvim were seen wrapped in an intimate embrace (*Yumah*, 54b, *Rashi* and *Ritva*, ad loc. *Medrash Eichah Rabba*, Pesichta, the Pirush *Yafah Anaf*. See *Likutei Sichos*, 21. p. 157, note 12. These were not the actual Keruvim, however, since during the First Temple period the Ark was hidden long before the Temple was destroyed. During the Second Temple there was no Ark, so perhaps this refers to the Keruvim that were embroidered on the *Paroches* / partition between the Holy and Holy of Holies).

We may deduce from this poetic image that the embrace of the Keruvim took place the moment before the separation, like two lovers who embrace passionately before they part ways. This is akin to moments of intense emotion expressed in the airport as spouses, friends or relatives say their tearful goodbyes before embarking on a long trip.

On a deeper level, this intense embrace can occur at the peak of the state of separation itself. For example, when your partner or child is living with you, their presence may seem routine and the expressions of affection between you may be less intense. If they needed to go away for a week, however, this may look very different. The first three days could go by easily, as you have still seen your loved one very recently. The last three days could be even easier, as you are closer to their return than to their departure. The hardest day, the day you would feel the most separation, yearning and affection, would therefore be the fourth day, the midpoint of the week. This is the day that you are furthest from both their departure and their return. This very distance has the power to elicit your most passionate affection and desire. Thus, the greater the sense of separation, the greater the revelation of unity.

Mutual yearning created by distance reveals a strong, intimate connection. The depths of separation coincide with the heights of togetherness. This is why, from within the insatiable yearning of exile and Cheser, the moment of the destruction of the Temple on Tisha b'Av is the very moment in which the soul of Moshiach is conceived.

☽

THE FULL MOON OF LOVE

Just as intense desire is revealed when lovers part, fiery passion manifests when they reunite after a period of prolonged absence. The pain of separation creates a yearning for uninterrupted union. When lovers triumphantly return to each other, they realize that their separation and exile was in fact illusory. Within their yearning, they were actually closer than ever before; except now their closeness is outwardly manifest. Tu b'Av is the day when Divine and human lovers triumphantly reunite. Their passionate love is illuminatingly revealed like the resplendent full moon.

The Medrash (*Eicha Rabbah*, 1:33. See also, *Ta'anis*, 29a, *Rashi* and *Tosefos*, ad loc. *Baba Basra*, 122a, *Rashi* and *Tosefos* ad loc) tells a striking story about Tu b'Av. It had been decreed that the generation of the Exodus would have to pass away in the Desert before the Children of Israel could enter the Holy Land. Every year on the Ninth of Av, Moshe (or a heavenly voice) would solemnly announce to the people, "Go and dig your graves." They would then dig graves for themselves and lie down in them for the night. When morning came, Moshe (a voice) would announce, "Arise, and separate the living from the dead." Those whose time had not yet come would get up and bury the dead. (Notice that the people 'heard' the voice instructing them to go dig their graves, and to separate themselves from the dead; the sense of hearing, as explored earlier, is intimately connected to the month of Av.)

When the morning of Tu b'Av arrived in the 39th year of traveling through the Desert, the entire community awoke and arose from their graves. Not one person had died, so they said, "It appears that we have made a mistake in our calculations. Perhaps this was not the night of the Ninth." To make sure, they repeated the funerary ritual on subsequent nights, and still no one died. Finally, on the night of the 15th, they saw the full moon and rejoiced: "The decree is over!" They then declared the 15th of Av a holiday (See *Rashi* and *Tosefos, Ta'anis*, 29a, and *Baba Basra*, 122a, in the name of the Medrash).

It is interesting to note that the people actually stopped dying on Tisha b'Av, but this was only conclusively revealed to them on Tu b'Av, the day of the full moon, when what had been previously concealed became revealed. Tu b'Av thus celebrates the open revelation of goodness hidden within the destruction of Tisha b'Av.

THE INNER REASON FOR THE
CELEBRATION OF TU B'AV:

Let us take a closer look at the meaning of Tu b'Av: "*There were no greater days of joy than Tu b'Av and Yom Kippur...On these days the daughters of Jerusalem would go out in white garments which they had borrowed, in order not to shame anyone who had none. The daughters of Jerusalem came out and danced in the vineyards, exclaiming, 'Young man, lift up your eyes and see what you choose for yourself!'*"

Our Sages offer six reasons for the celebratory nature of this day:

It is the day on which permission was granted to the Tribes of Israel to intermarry with each other (originally, one was only allowed to marry within his or her own tribe).

It is the day on which the tribe of *Binyamin* / Benjamin was permitted to re-enter the congregation of Israel. (Following a terrible episode that had occurred concerning the tribe of Binyamin, a ban had been placed upon marrying into their tribe.)

It is the day on which the Israelites conclusively realized that the generation that had left *Mitzrayim* / Egypt had ceased dying in the Wilderness.

It is the day on which *Hoshea* / Hosea removed the guards which *Yerovam* / Jeroboam had placed on the roads to prevent Israel from going up to Jerusalem on pilgrimage.

It is the day on which permission was granted to bury those killed at the massacre of Beitar.

It was the annual day on which Temple workers stopped felling trees for the service of the altar. From the 15th of Av onwards, the strength of the sun grows less and the wood of the felled trees would not dry sufficiently. (In the summer, they would allow the hot sun to dry out felled trees, so that no creatures would reside within them. The wood had to be clean of all living creatures before being used on the Altar.) Thus they called this day, "the Day of the Breaking of the Axe".

That is what we find in the Gemara, according to the teachings of the Sages. Being that the first two reasons above are connected with marriage — the intermarrying of the tribes and the tribe of Binyamin being permitted to re-enter and marry the other tribes — it became a day dedicated to finding a spouse.

Additionally, a deeper reading of these six reasons reveals that they are all connected to the idea of *Lashuv* / to return and *Yichud* / unification and reunification. These ideas are the basic themes of marriage: to return two separate 'half' souls to a unified whole.

The permission granted to the tribes to inter-marry is a concept of *Yichud,* the unity of Klal Yisrael.

The permission granted to the tribe of Binyamin to re-enter the congregation of Israel represents the ideas of *Yichud* as well as *Lashuv.*

When the generation of the wilderness ceased dying unnaturally, the community 'returned to life'.

When Hoshea removed the guards on the road to Yerushalayim, Klal Yisrael could return to the *Makom haMikdash* / place of the Temple. The place of the Mikdash is the essential point within all of space (*Bereishis*, 28:11; *Rashi* ad loc) and the place of our collective birth (*Medrash Rabba*, Bereishis, 14:8. *Pirkei d'Rebbe Eliezer*, 12), and thus a return to this place is a return to our essential nature.

When permission was granted to bury the victims of Beitar, it represented a return of the body to its natural habitat, the earth: "From dust you came and to dust you shall return."

When they stopped felling trees for the altar, they were free to learn Torah, as seems clear from the Gemara. As the days get shorter, the nights become longer, and "the nights were created to study Torah" (*ibid*). This is a spiritual return to immersion in Torah, the teaching of Divine Unity.

The Sages call Tu b'Av a *Yom Tov* / a day of goodness or holiday. In a traditional sense, *Yom Tov* means a festival day during which it is forbidden to do work (Rambam, *Hilchos Yom Tov*, 1:1). On Tu b'Av, however, work is permitted. While other non-festival celebratory days are also called *Yom Tov* (See *Yuma*, 70a), with regards to Tu b'Av there is a special reason. Adam and Chavah were originally created as a single, unified being called *haAdam* / the earth-being. Hashem saw that the masculine dimension of that being was lonely and said, "It is not good for *haAdam* to be alone" (*Bereishis*, 2:18), and then separated Chavah out as an individual. This was the beginning of the first human relationship. The condition of being alone is called 'not good', and being in relationship with another is called 'good'. Tu b'Av is thus called a 'good day' as it is a day of returning to unity through marriage and relationship. (*Note, the idea of *Tov* / good is also related to the burial of the victims of Beitar, *Berachos*, 48b. And ultimate Tov is the soul's return to the state beyond death, period. *Avodah Zarah*, 5a).

'Good' refers to unity, and the opposite of good is *Ra* / bad. The word *Ra* comes from the word *Reu'a* / shaky, unstable, uncertain, broken. Tu b'Av is a 'good' day because it is a day of finding love, making stable connections and returning to wholeness.

The Medrash (*Pesikta*) teaches that in the future, the seven days from Tisha b'Av through Tu b'Av will be a seven day holiday, similar to the seven Biblical days of Pesach. In this way, Tu b'Av is essentially connected to the final day of Pesach, the day of the Splitting of the Sea. Our Sages teach, "To match couples is as difficult as the Splitting of the Sea" (*Sotah*, 2a). Just as the Splitting of the Sea opens the waters to reveal the traversable ground within the deepest depths, finding a spouse demands an opening and revealing of the deepest depths of the soul. The quality of Tu b'Av helps one to reveal and reconnect to the roots of their soul, which allows one to identify and unite with one's soulmate.

❧

TU B'AV AND YOM KIPPUR

"There were no greater days of Yom Tov than Tu b'Av and Yom Kippur." Why is that? One deeper link between the two holidays is that if not for the episode of the Golden Calf, Tu b'Av would have been Yom Kippur. How so? If not for the Golden Calf, each of the months of the year would have had a Yom Tov (*Yalkut Shimoni*, Pinchas, 782). The month of Nisan would have had the Yom Tov of Pesach, and the month of Iyyar the Yom Tov of *Pesach Katan* / Small Pesach. The month of Sivan would have had the Yom Tov of Shavuos, and the month of Tamuz would have had a *Yom Tov Gadol* / a great Yom Tov — perhaps Rosh Hashanah. According to this sequence, the month of Av would contain the next sequential Yom Tov, Yom Kippur. Elul would then have Sukkos, and Tishrei would have Shemini Atzeres. But because of the *Kilkul* / breakdown that led to the worshiping of the Golden Calf and the resultant smashing of the Luchos, the holidays from the months of Tamuz Av, and Elul were all moved to Tishrei. This is one of the deeper reasons behind the Sages' spiritual juxtaposition of Tu b'Av and Yom Kippur.

☾

A TIME OF DIVINE DESIRE

We have explored our Sages' six primary reasons for Tu b'Av being considered a Yom Tov, as well as the spiritual theme underlying these reasons, 'returning to unity'. The question still remains: why was this specific day chosen to lift the ban on intermarriage between the tribes, and to allow the reentry of the tribe of Binyamin?

What is the inner quality of Tu b'Av that gives rise to the six events that occurred on this day?

Tu b'Av is unique in that it is the day when the Divine desire was aroused to create a world, to create relationship with an 'other'. For this reason it is a day of forging the deepest bonds and uniting with another person.

☾

LONGING FOR LOVE

Rosh Hashanah is colloquially called the 'Birthday of the World'. But in fact, Rosh Hashanah represents the Sixth Day of Creation: the day Hashem created Humanity. Therefore, the First Day of Creation falls five days earlier, on the 25th of Elul. Clearly, there can be no 'time' before the creation of time, and there was no month of Elul or 25th day before the moon and the sun were created; however, we may explore this teaching on a conceptual level.

There is a debate among the Sages regarding the date of the birth of humanity. Rabbi Eliezer argues that the creation of humanity was on the first day of the month of Tishrei, on Rosh Hashanah. Rabbi Yehoshua, however, asserts that it was the first day of the month of Nisan (*Rosh Hashanah*, 11a). The Arizal reconciles these opinions saying that the 'pregnancy' begins on the First of Tishrei, and the actual 'birth' occurs on the First of Nisan.

In the Rosh Hashanah liturgy, in the sentence, *HaYom Haras Olam* / Today a world is born, the word *Haras* comes from the word *Hirayon* / pregnancy. Therefore, a more literal translation might read, 'Today is the pregnancy of the world'. The actual 'birth' of the world then occurs seven months later, in the month of Nisan (*Pri Eitz Chayim*, Shar HaShofar, 5. *Ben Yehoyada*, Rosh Hashanah, 10b). This interpretation is similar to a comment by Tosefos (*Rosh Hashanah*, 27a) explaining that the 'thought' of creating humanity entered the Creator's mind in Tishrei, whereas the actual Creation took place six months later, in Nisan.

On Rosh Hashanah, the world and human beings begin to take shape within the mind of the Creator, like a fetus within the womb of the mother. Tishrei begins the autumn and winter months, when the life-force of nature retreats into concealment, like a child in utero, hidden from view but actively growing nonetheless. Then, the world and human beings are born in the month of Nisan. Nisan inaugurates the spring and summer seasons, when the life force of nature is again revealed as the world blossoms and blooms. If Rosh Hashanah is when humanity is formed as a fetus within the womb of the Creator, as it were, then the 25th of Elul is when the world as a whole begins to emerge as a developing fetus.

The day of Tu b'Av falls 40 days before the 25th of Elul. What is the significance of these 40 days? According to Torah law it takes 40 days from the moment of conception for a human embryo to become an actual fetus (*Niddah*, 30a. *Kerisus*, 10a. See also: *Berachos*, 60a. *Sotah*, 2a). At around 40 days, a heartbeat appears and the fetus is considered a complete living being. Forty days before the 25th of Elul is the 15th day of the month prior to Elul — the 15th of Av. Tu b'Av is therefore the moment of the *conception* of the world, which then develops and reveals its form as a viable creation on the 25th of Elul.

Tu b'Av thus embodies the first 'conscious' stirring of Divine love, the first movement within the Creator's Mind to create an 'other'. This is the day when there first arose a Divine desire and longing to create an earthly 'child', that is, a world with sentient beings who will eventually come into relationship with their beloved Heavenly Parent. Tu b'Av is therefore the moment of initial conception, the moment of intimate embrace and the first loving 'twinkle in the eye' of the Parent for the child, which will be formed 40 days later and eventually born in the Spring.

In the Torah, the number 40 symbolizes transformation. It took 40 days for the Great Flood to cleanse the world, preparing it to be recreated. It took 40 years of traveling through the Desert for a group of slaves to be transformed into a free people. Hashem's first stirring of love and *Cheishek* / desire, resulting in the conception of Creation, is eventually transformed into a living reality 40 days later, on the 25th of Elul, when the 'fetus' of the world is formed and viable.

The days of the calendar from Tu b'Av through Adar represent various stages of prenatal development leading up to the birth of this 'child' in Nisan. But, truthfully, even before conception, the seven days between Tisha b'Av and Tu b'Av are also part of this process. These seven days are full of the euphoric expectation of a single person who has just heard the news that they are about to meet their destined beloved. We anticipate this first Divine meeting with great longing, excitement and hope. A whole new world of love is about to unfold. There is about to be a connection, a conception, a pregnancy and eventually the birth of a beautiful child.

That child is you. That child is a shining new world of infinite possibility.

When Tu b'Av arrives, it is thus the moment of generative intimacy between Divinity and humanity. The great *Cheshek* / desire prior to this moment brings about such a cosmic conception. This is the deep, inner reason why Tu b'Av was chosen as the archetypal day of human intimacy and renewed hope for the future, as the world below mirrors the world above. On every level, therefore, Tu b'Av is the day of intimate unification that initiates a new creation.

€

DANCING ALONE OR WITH OTHERS:
Holy vs. Unholy Dance

As mentioned, Tu b'Av is the paradigmatic time of relationships, both between Creator and creation, as well as between people. This relational dynamic is best understood as a kind of dance. As we know, Tisha b'Av is the day when both Temples were destroyed, but it was on the 17th of Tamuz that the walls of *Yerushalayim* / Jerusalem were breached. Such profound brokenness is rooted in the episode of Moshe coming down from Mount Sinai on the 17th of Tamuz only to witness the Israelites worshipping the Golden Calf; upon such a sight, Moshe smashed the *Luchos* / Tablets that he was bringing down to the people.

A closer reading of this episode reveals that Moshe did not break the Luchos only because he saw the Israelites serving the idol, as he was aware of this before. Rather, when he came down the mountain and saw them 'dancing', only then did he smash the Luchos. As the verse says: "Now it came to pass when he drew closer to the camp and saw the calf and the *dances*...he flung the tablets from his hands, shattering them at the foot of the mountain" (*Shemos* 32:19). What does dancing represent in this context? What was distinct about the kind of dancing he witnessed in that moment? And how does this dancing on the 17th of Tamuz relate to the dancing of Tu b'Av? For, as the Mishna says: "There were no greater days of joy than Tu b'Av and Yom Kippur. On these days, the daughters of Jerusalem would go out in white garments which each had borrowed in order not to shame anyone who had none. They *danced* in the vineyards, exclaiming, 'Young man, lift up your eyes and see what you choose for yourself'" (Mishnah, *Ta'anis* 4:8). Somehow these two episodes of dancing are connected and contrasted; the question is, how?

At the end of the Talmudic tractate of Ta'anis, which speaks in great detail about the laws and practices of fasting, including the history and the laws of the 17th of Tamuz and Tisha b'Av, there is the following teaching: "In the future, Hashem will make a circle of Tzadikim in the Garden of Eden, and Hashem will sit inside the circle. The Tzadikim will dance and point towards the center of the circle, and declare: 'This is our G-d for whom we have waited, that He might save us. This is Hashem for whom we hoped, we will be glad and rejoice in His salvation'" (*Ta'anis*, 31a, quoting *Yeshayahu*, 25:9). And so, the entire episode of destruction begins with a dance, the wild dance around the Golden Calf; and Redemption, too, is symbolized by another (different) dance, the circle dance of the Sages.

Still, the question remains unanswered: What is the connection between these days and dances?

It is clear from these teachings that there is an unholy form of dance — not only defined by the venue and situation within which it is occurring — and there is a holy form of dance. The fundamental difference between the two is whether the dance is purely self-centered or if it is in relationship with others.

Unholy dance is solitary and selfishly oriented; holy dance occurs in a larger group, with each individual holding someone else's hand, rejoicing together in a revolving circle.

A marked distinction between the Golden Calf and (l'havdil) the sacred Keruvim that were placed in the Holy of Holies (besides the fact that, as the *Kuzari* points out, the Golden Calf was a product of the people's limited projection, whereas the Keruvim were fashioned according to the Divine command of the Torah) is that one is singular and the other is dual, and thus capable of relationship. The Golden Calf was a 'male image', created by 'males' (the men in the Desert forcefully ripped off the gold jewelry from their wives to create it), and worshiped by males.*

The Keruvim, on the other hand, were two entities fashioned in a 'male and female' form (*Yuma*, 54a), suggesting a relationship. Two-ness thus represents going outside of oneself and reaching out to another in order to connect. This fundamental relational dynamic,

---

* Even according to the Arizal, who maintains that the Calf was actually a 'male and female' image, it was still only an image of male and female positioned *Achar b'Achor* / back to back, i.e., as "one entity", incapable of a face-to-face encounter or exchange. Arizal, *Sha'ar Maamorei Rashbi*, Mishpatim. *Sha'ar Hapesukim*, Ekev.

by association, ultimately implies reaching out to the Holy Other in order to cleave to Hashem alone.

A solitary dance, meant solely to impress others, or even one that is simply self-absorbed, is essentially unholy, and has the potential to cut one off from their Source, from their community and ultimately from themselves on the deepest level. When Moshe came down the mountain, he knew already that the Israelites were worshiping an idol; but when he saw the depth of their egocentric self-indulgence, he became worried that there was no longer any hope for these men. They had sunk so low that he feared they were incapable of ever returning and reaching out to the Transcendent One. He observed in that moment that they were completely stuck within themselves, exemplified by the fact that they were worshiping a deity based on their own reflection who was in reality created to serve them, as idol-worshipers 'stand on top' of their idols (*Bereishis Rabba*, 69:3). And so — he smashed the Luchos. The *Tikkun /* rectification for this type of self-centered dance is the contrasting feminine dance of unity and connection; this is an other-centered dance, where the women would dance in the vineyard in order to attract a mate and enter into an intimate relationship.

The ultimate Tikkun will come when the Tzadikim (perhaps referring to 'elevated males'), will dance together in a *Machol /* circle, and in addition to this other-centered collective dance, they will actually point to the Holy Other, and acknowledge the transcendent presence of Hashem in their midst.

The word *Machol /* circle is related to the word *Mechilah /* forgiveness, which is perhaps further related to the words *Lach /* fluid or wet, *Chol* / sand, or *Chalal* / empty (like a tube). In a circle dance, everyone joins hands; and in order for the dancers to remain in harmony, everyone in the circle must be in sync and in rhythm with the entire group. A person, therefore, needs to empty himself and become fluid, receptive and responsive to other people's rhythms for the circle to remain whole and unbroken.

Remaining stuck within oneself and dancing purely to one's own drummer, with no consideration for the presence and position of anyone else, is emblematic of idol (self) worship. The opposite of this self-obsessed dynamic is to dance with others in a *Machol* / circle. In order to do this, one must practice *Mechilah* / *forgiveness* as learning to dance with others requires one to be a bit more fluid and forgiving of other people's missteps. Ultimately, it is through this very humbling and clumsy process and practice of learning to dance with others, where one learns how to dance with and reach out to Hashem, the Ultimate Other.

The circle dance is a living example of the deeper concept of dynamic *Yichud* / unity, which is the great Tikkun for all the self-centeredness and disunity that caused the Temples' destruction in the first place. Additionally, this concept of unity is the spiritual foundation underlying all six of the previously explored events that epitomize the energy of Tu b'Av, a day focused entirely on creating healthy connections with others.

When we are able to be a bit more fluid and practice Mechilah with others as we dance with them in a Machol, Hashem will surely return that goodwill gesture by extending a full Mechilah to us for all of our missteps. This Divine forgiveness will eventually uproot and repair all the prior destructions, bringing forth the revelation of our righteous Moshiach and initiating the rebuilding of the Third Holy Temple, speedily in our days.

€

TU B'AV & THE TIKKUN FOR TISHA B'AV: *Three Levels of Meaning*

LEVEL ONE

"There were (and *are*) no greater days of joy as Tu b'Av and Yom Kippur." Tu b'Av is set aside as a day of joy because of the six meta-historical events mentioned earlier. Each of these six events are defined, at their root, by an overriding energy of spiritual returning and revealing of *Yichud* / unity. However, Tu b'Av is *most essentially* a day of joy because, as we explored, it is the day of the ultimate Yichud: the intimate encounter between human and Divine, and the resulting conception of the world and ourselves. On this day of the Divine 'conception' of the world, there is an extra spiritual flow of love, making it an opportune moment to seek out and open oneself to love and connection with others. Ultimately, it is love that returns us to integral relationship and holistic unity. The world is founded on love and the desire to connect with, and relate to, an 'other'. Our very being is based on the Divine love that brought us into being. Therefore, since it is love that brings about Yichud, all of the six meta-historical events, which are but individual expressions of the essential energy of the day, are each related to some form of Yichud.

Based on this understanding, it becomes clear that the link between Tisha b'Av and Tu b'Av is teleological, as one is intended to move from one state into another. The existential state of dejection, alienation, separation, poverty and exile that one experiences on Tisha b'Av is meant to bring one to a higher state of love, unity and Redemption. The emptier the vessel, the more it can be filled. The lower the point one falls to, the higher the peak one may climb. Tu b'Av occurs on the full moon, symbolizing the 'revelation' that despite all of our apparent lowliness, emptiness and exile, Hashem is always fully present in Yichud with us — no matter how splintered or eclipsed we may feel. Hashem is always fully in love with us, just like that moment we 'first met' under the light of the full moon. Despite our 'poverty' and borrowed garments, we boldly called out: 'Lift up Your eyes and see, Hashem, what You choose for Yourself!'

Level Two

On another level, Tu b'Av is not only a revelation and continuation of Tisha b'Av, but it is actually a Tikkun for the effects of the events of Tisha b'Av. The effects of the *Churban* / destruction were, and are, separation on every level: communal, geographical and spiritual. The People were no longer at home in their homeland. Correspondingly, on Tisha b'Av we focus on our feelings of separation from the true depth and authenticity within us.

Another essential effect of the Churban is a sense of loss and defeat in the present that arises in contrast to a glorified past. Bemoaning the Churban necessarily includes contemplating our spiritually elevated state before the Churban, when the Temple stood and we were whole in our Land. In fact, the very construct of a 'past' is synonymous with 'loss' and exile. Yechezkel's vision in the beginning of the Exile begins with him sitting by the banks of the River Kevar when the spirit of Prophecy descends upon him. The name *Kevar* literally means 'already'. We can understand this to mean that he was in exile *because* he was sitting along the banks of 'the River of Already', gazing at the 'waters' of the past, dwelling on what once was and now is gone. Exile is a burdensome clinging to what has been. Focusing on an extinct past robs us of the freedom to experience newness and to create movement in the present.

After the Churban, many of the men were so plagued by the recent past, and their traumas weighed so heavily upon them, that they held that Jews should stop having children: "Since the day of the destruction of the Temple we should by right bind ourselves not to eat meat nor drink wine...nor to marry and have children" (*Baba Basra*, 60b). This is an extreme example of being stuck in the pain of the past and thereby allowing it to fossilize your future.

We need to mourn and be present with the full pain of exile, but sometimes mourning can be too overwhelming. Grief can overtake a person and completely cloud over the possibility of a brighter tomorrow. It can be tempting to give up on the future, as it may require real work, both spiritual and physical, to turn things around. And here is precisely where Tu b'Av can be the right Tikkun and perfect healing for the deleterious effects of Tisha b'Av.

Whereas the men were paralyzed, ceaselessly dwelling on the tragedy of what had already occurred, and were even considering giving up completely, the women called to them, 'Young men, lift up your eyes! Let's start thinking about rebuilding, about starting a family, about creating a brighter future.' It is a great *Nechamah* / comfort to release the past, and to give oneself the inner permission to return to life and start rebuilding.

"There were no greater Yom Tovs than Yom Kippur and Tu b'Av." The juxtaposition of these two holidays highlights their common theme: they both encourage a release from the past. On Yom Kippur, we are forgiven and released from the effects of our own negative past actions. On Tu b'Av, we are released from the darkness and collective trauma of our people's history. On both days, we are given the ability to start anew.

On Tu b'Av, it is the *Nekeivah* / female who says to the *Zachar* / male: "Lift up your eyes" — 'Come, see the possibility of a *future*; let's get married and build a home.' *Zachar* / male is from the word *Zachor* / memory, suggesting a tendency to dwell on the past. *Nekeivah* / female comes from the world *Nekev* / opening, suggesting the openness necessary to move into the future. Another word for 'woman' is *Isha,* from the word *Noshe* / forgetting, allowing one to let go of the past and move on.

Sometimes it is good to remember, and sometimes it is good to forget. In this case, the paradigmatic masculine assertion is that in order to be realistic, we must maintain an acute memory of the past. The archetypal feminine suggests that in order to go on living, we need to let go of the past, look to the future and create a new beginning. From this perspective, the male is preoccupied with the "past" and thus in a place of perpetual Churban. This is the wounded masculine quality that is epitomized on Tisha b'Av. Then, along comes the female and says to the male: "Lift up your eyes!" 'Let's return to the present and focus on the future! Let's marry, have children and build our lives together, instead of being stuck in the past and bemoaning what once "was". This is the feminine voice that calls us forward into the future on Tu b'Av.

When Moshe came down the mountain on the 17th of Tamuz and saw the people worshipping the Golden Calf, he broke the *Luchos* / Tablets written by Hashem Himself. Many centuries later, this was the very day when the walls of Jerusalem were breached, beginning the process of Churban and exile. As is clear in the Torah, the erection of the Golden Calf was initiated by men, created by men and worshipped by men. The women did not participate. This gendered trend continues in the episode of the *Meraglim* / scouts sent by Moshe to report back to the people about the Promised Land. But how?

The people cried in self-defeat when they heard the frightening, negative reports of the *Meraglim*. It was then decreed that this generation would not enter Israel, but would die in the wilderness; and henceforward, this day would become a day of wailing for future generations. Many centuries later, on this day, the Churban of Tisha b'Av occurred. But it all began with the Meraglim, who were, of course, all men.

The Pasuk / verse states: "Send for yourself spies, men..." (*Bamidbar*, 13:2). Commenting on this verse, Rashi says, "It is *up to you* to send them (*Rashi*, ad loc); i.e., 'It's your decision to send the men.' The Kli Yakar then interprets Rashi's comment in a very interesting way that connects with the gendered nature of Tisha b'Av and Tu b'Av: Hashem told Moshe, 'If I had it My way, I would send women – not men. The women have shown a strong desire for the Holy Land.' According to this teaching, it becomes clear that: if the chosen scouts would have been women, they would have come back with a positive, hopeful report to strengthen and inspire the people. And therefore, in fact, the women were not part of the decreed punishment that was brought about and caused because of the Meraglim (*Tanchumah*, Pinchas, 7. *Rashi*, Bamidbar, 26:64).

Again, we notice the whole reason for the Churban is connected to men specifically, and not to the women. Furthermore, the ultimate Redemption and eventual rebuilding of the Temple is also connected to and dependent upon the rectified role of women.

According to the Chidushei haRim, the seven days from the Ninth of Av until the fifteenth of Av parallel the seven days of *Shivah* / mourning period of one who has lost a close relative. So, beginning on Tisha b'Av, we embrace the sadness, sensitize ourselves to loss and mourn our glorious past. Then, after we have 'sat Shivah' for seven days, the feminine principle comes along and says, 'Listen to me. Today is the day we need to get up from this pit! Don't just focus on lowliness and destruction. Lift up your eyes! You're a "young man", you have a future, you have "choice" — choose life! Let's envision the highest reality possible, let's imagine what we can build together — let's start right now, let's write a guest list for our wedding! What beautiful children we will have! What a beautiful life we have ahead of us!'

On a deeper level, the marriage and the children that are born out of this love are triggers that hasten the coming of the ultimate Redemption (*Yevamos*, 62a) — the 'beautiful life' of the 'future'. For this reason, the Mishnah (*Ta'anis*) which speaks about Tu b'Av concludes with a description of the ultimate wedding between us and Hashem. The Talmudic commentary on this Mishnah, and on the conclusion of the entire tractate of Ta'anis which discusses the laws and practices of fast days, concludes with a glimpse of this love-infused 'future'. As explored earlier, the Talmud speaks about a time when "Hashem will make a *Machol* / circle dance (related to the word *Mechilah* / total forgiveness) for the Tzadikim. Hashem will, so to speak, sit among the Tzadikim in Gan Eden, and they will point with their finger and say, "…This is Hashem for Whom we have waited. We will be glad and rejoice in His salvation!" (*Ta'anis*, 31a). This Messianic circle dance is, as previously noted, also connected with these gendered dynamics, as the form of the dance itself is understood as expressing a feminine quality. Indeed, the hastening of Redemption is intimately tied to the rectification of misaligned masculine energy, which also keeps us paralyzed in the pain of the past, and the ability to responsibly integrate the feminine quality, which beckons us into a future full of infinite possibility.

LEVEL THREE

On the deepest level, Tu b'Av is the Tikkun for the root of the Churban itself, not only for its effects. As we have mentioned, there were two major events in the *Midbar* / Desert directly tied to the Churban. One is the *Cheit haEigel* / Sin of the Golden Calf, which led Moshe to smash the Luchos, and the other is the episode with the *Meraglim* / Scouts and their negative report, which caused the people to lose faith in their mission and cry out in premature defeat. The Cheit haEigel is specifically connected with our fast on the 17th of Tamuz, and the episode of the Meraglim is connected with Tisha b'Av. These two catastrophic events are the two bookends of The Three Weeks, which begin on the 17th of Tamuz and conclude on the 9th of Av.

The general consensus (see, the *Beis HaLevi*, Bo) is that the Cheit haEigel was an issue of *Avodah Zarah* / idol worship, and the Cheit of the Meraglim was an issue of *Cheser Emunah* / lack of faith in Hashem. The Beis HaLevi (ibid) also ties these two episodes to the destructions of the First and Second Beis haMikdash. The First was destroyed because of Avodah Zarah and the Second because of *Sinas Chinam* / senseless hatred (*Yuma*, 9b). Hatred in general, he explains, as well as this specific incidence of strife among Klal Yisrael, are both rooted in a lack of faith in the Sages. Since Klal Yisrael did not have Emunah in the Sages and stopped adhering to them, the community became decentralized and splintered into factions. This atmosphere of separation and disagreement eventually led to hatred and enmity between people.

There is faith in Hashem, which the Meraglim apparently lacked. There is also faith in the *Chachamim* / Sages, which Klal Yisrael lacked at the time of the Churban of the Second Beis haMikdash. And then, there is Emunah in oneself and in one's capabilities. These three types of Emunah are deeply linked. In fact, all Emunah begins with self-confidence and faith in oneself. When you have confidence and faith in yourself, you are open to have faith in others — as what you see in others is a reflection of yourself. When you have faith in yourself, you can also have genuine faith in the Creator of your life. The root of all ills and all 'sins' is the lack of faith in oneself. Once you give up on yourself, nothing matters any longer.

While the story of the Meraglim is, on its surface, about a lack of faith in Hashem, this condition began with the scouts' lack of faith in themselves. The Meraglim were chosen for their mission because they were the heads of the tribes, and thus considered "men of distinction". One of the deeper reasons they were actively looking to see negativity in the Land is: they secretly wished to stay sheltered in the protective cocoon of the Clouds of Glory, shielded and guided as they were by the Divine pillar of fire and fed with the food of the angels. To them, it seemed spiritually impossible to live with the intense physicality of the Land, as the Land would need to be plowed, worked and built up. Because they lacked spiritual confidence in themselves, they also projected their lack of confidence onto Hashem. They even thought it would be impossible for Hashem to take them into the Land.

This lack of confidence in their spiritual potential seeped into their very identity. They began to reject faith, even in themselves. When they said that they had seen mighty giants in the Land, it was somewhat understandable, even if an exaggeration. But when they said "...and we were in their eyes like grasshoppers" (*Bamidbar*, 13:33), how could they have known how they looked in *their* eyes? If you think you are worthless, dispensable or as lowly as a grasshopper, you will start imagining that everyone else around you sees you in the same light. You will thus project your own damaged self-image onto the world and assume this is how the world sees you, not realizing that it is only how you see yourself!

Earlier, a Medrash was quoted that recounts how each year on Tisha b'Av, Moshe (or a voice) would announce to the people, "Go and dig your graves"; and they would then spend the night buried in the earth, prepared for the worst. Many people would indeed die each year on that night. Until one year, no one died. So they said, "Perhaps that was not actually the night of the Ninth", and they repeated the ritual. They continued each night until the night of the 15th, when they saw the full moon and knew for certain that the Ninth of Av had passed. When they realized that the decree of death was over, they rejoiced.

What actually happened is that on the night of Tu b'Av, they regained their confidence. They realized that Hashem was with them, and that it was possible for them to enter the Land. They had actually stopped dying on the Ninth of Av, but only celebrated that fact on the 15th, since that was when they finally regained their faith. Up until that point, they were in such a dark place that they did not even believe in the possibility that they could live. As a result, all they could imagine was that maybe they made the wrong calculation. *There must be some mistake!* But in the beautiful words of the Rambam, "Only then (on the 15th) were *t*hey confident in themselves, and they believed in themselves, and they felt the will of the Creator and the passing of the Divine wrath from upon them" (*Pirush haMishnayos*, Ta'anis, at the end).

The root of the mishap with the Meraglim, and thus all the tragedies of Tisha b'Av, was a lack of faith in oneself leading to a lack of faith in the Sages, and ultimately to a lack of faith in Hashem. We can make a Tikkun for all of this on Tu b'Av when we listen to the voice of hope, and regain our spiritual confidence in ourselves to build a brighter future for the coming generations. Tu b'Av is therefore a time "to deepen faith in oneself" which, as discussed, is the root of faith in others as well as in Hashem (*Ritva*, ibid).

ॐ

PRACTICE: LISTENING

*A*S DISCUSSED, THE SECOND HALF OF THE MONTH, beginning on Tu b'Av, is about finding love and being open to the possibility of new relationship. Additionally, the sense corresponding to the entire month is hearing. These two themes are intricately related. But, how?

The foundation of every relationship is open communication. Our Sages offer a definition of a person with whom one is quarreling: "a person with whom you have not spoken to for three days because of your anger with him" (*Sanhedrin*, 27b). Yet, as explored, really communicating with someone is not merely speaking 'at' them, nor passively accepting what they are saying. True communication requires listening deeply in such a way that an actual bond is forged. The Tikkun of this month includes deep listening, and creating the possibility of deeply relating to an 'other'. This is, therefore, a good month to work on repairing fissures of separation within our relationships.

Practice reaching out to someone with whom you have experienced distance or have not truly listened to in a while. Choose someone with whom you have lost positive contact — perhaps a parent, sibling or community member. Listen to the hidden good within them. Open yourself to the possibility of a sensitive and supportive relationship.

The word *Moshiach* resembles the word *Mesiach* / communicator. When we communicate openly and authentically, we create the conditions for reconciliation and reunion. This is a taste of Moshiach that we can experience in the here and now. May we merit to listen and speak to each other in such a way that we are able to see and experience the full revelation of Moshiach and the Redemption of the entire world, speedily in our days.

ใ๊

SUMMARY OF AV
The 12 Dimensions of Av

12 Dimensions of Av	
Sequence of Hashem's Name	Hei-Vav-Yud-Hei
Torah Verse	"Hinei Yad Hashem **HoYah** / Behold, the hand of Hashem is upon…"(*Shemos*, 9:3); or, alternatively: "**Hashkes U-shema Yisrael Hayom** / Keep silent and hear Israel, today… (*Devarim*, 27:9)
Letter	Tes (ט)
Month Name	*Menachem Av* ('Comforting Father')
Sense	Hearing
Zodiac	*Aryeh* / the Lion, or Leo
Tribe	Shimon
Body Part	Left Kidney
Element	Fire
Parshios	Beginning of *Sefer Devarim* or Deuteronomy
Season	Summer
Holiday	Tisha b'Av (9th of Av), Tu b'Av (15th of Av)

SUMMARY

I N THE MONTH OF AV, THE INTENSE HEAT OF THE SUMMER season peaks and subtly abates, stimulating an energy of *Ta'avah* / desire or lust. To rectify the destructive fire of lust, it must be transformed into a non-destructive, illuminating fire; *Aish* / fire is the **element** of the month. In order to thus elevate *Ta'avah* to its root, we must harness the **sense** of the month, *Shmi'a* / hearing, and listen to the deeper spiritual yearning behind our physical desires. We also need to employ the qualities of the left kidney, the **body part** of the month, which extracts the good elements in our blood from the bad, allowing us to purify and refine our passions.

The devouring fire of lustful desires destroys relationships and creates suffering. The **sign** of the month is *Aryeh* / the Lion, alluding to the Holy Temples, which were destroyed by fire on Tisha b'Av (the first **holiday** of the month). The **verse** of the month contains a cry of 'Woe!' This alludes to the practices of mourning that we must engage in throughout the beginning of the month, in order to 'hear' and embrace the suffering and destruction present throughout our history, and in our lives. The emotional vulnerability of mourning is the necessary first step in extracting and revealing the deeper goodness hidden within suffering.

The **letter sequence of Hashem's Name** for this month begins with a direct reversal of the proper flow, and concludes with the last two letters in their proper alignment: Hei-Vav, Yud-Hei. This alludes to the harshness present throughout the beginning of the month, as well the great goodness and kindness that is revealed at the midpoint of the month, on the holiday of Tu b'Av. The **letter** of the month is Tes, alluding to the First Light of Creation, which is called *Tov*; this is the ultimate 'good' hidden even within destruction. Tu b'Av is this light hidden within the darkness of Tisha b'Av.

Menachem Av / Comforting Father, which is the **name** of the month, also alludes to the reversal of harshness and destruction, exemplified by the joy and connection revealed on Tu b'Av. In our personal *Avodah* / spiritual work, we can help to comfort others when we listen deeply to them. The **tribe** of the month, Shimon, comes from the word *Shema* / listen. Shimon listened deeply to Dina after she had been raped, bringing her some measure of comfort. The ultimate purpose of listening is to unify the speaker and listener, and reveal the Divine Oneness within the speaker. The

Parshios of this month, though inspired by Hashem, are spoken in the first person through the mouth of Moshe, demonstrating the ultimate Oneness of the Speaker and listener. May we merit to listen deeply to ourselves, to others and ultimately to Hashem, in order to transform our reality and reveal the Light of Redemption.

KAVANAH / Mindful Intention:

We hear on multiple levels: from simple physiological hearing, to deep listening in which we identify needs and empower the speaker. While the primary objective of listening is to benefit the other, it can also be used as a touchpoint for our own *Avodah /* spiritual work. For example, when we hear something we can ask ourselves, 'Why am I hearing this?' 'What can I learn from this?' 'What is the Divine message in this for me?'

A wise person is someone who learns from everyone (*Avos*, 4:1). Reb Simcha Bunim of Peshischa teaches (*Kol Simcha*, Vayetze) that every person needs a teacher to teach him Torah, and the way to serve Hashem. Yet, someone who is wise, meaning that they are able to learn from every person — even finding Divine teachings within mundane conversations — this person does not need one specific teacher, for everyone is his teacher.

Indeed, every person we encounter and every situation in which we find ourselves is a teacher designed specifically for us at that exact time and place. Everything is conspiring to teach us about ourselves, about the universe and ultimately about the Divine.

As a practice to deepen and expand your powers of deep listening, take a specific statement that you heard today. Sit with this statement for a few moments, and open yourself to hearing the inner mesSages between the lines of these words. Ask yourself how what you heard can help you become a better person, bringing you closer to yourself, to your loved ones and to Hashem? What is the message you needed to learn within what you heard?

APPENDIX

THE FIVE CALAMITIES OF TAMUZ / AV & PLAN A, B AND C FOR CREATION

There are five calamities mentioned by our Sages (at the end of trac-tate *Ta'anis*) that occurred on the first day of The Three Weeks, the 17th of Tamuz. There are also five calamities that occurred on the final day of The Three Weeks, the 9th of Av.

On the 17th of Tamuz:

1) Moshe, seeing the people worshiping and dancing around the Golden Calf, smashed the *Luchos* / Tablets.

2) During the Babylonian siege on Jerusalem in the First Temple Era, the Jews were forced to stop offering daily sacrifices due to a lack of cattle.

3) The leader of the Roman occupiers of Israel burned a Torah scroll.

4) An idol was placed in the Holy Temple.

5) The walls of Jerusalem were breached.

It is self-evident that these five events are not simply five random events that happened to occur on the same day years apart, but rath-er they are all intrinsically connected to the general theme of the 17th of Tamuz.

The first calamity listed above is the root of the other four. The sin of the Golden Calf caused the breaking of the Luchos — which opened the possibility of running out of cattle for offerings, the burning of the Torah, the placing of an idol in the Temple and the walls of the Holy City being breached.

On the 9th of Av:

1) The *Meraglim* / spies or scouts returned on this night to the Israelites in the Desert and relayed a grim report about the Land of Israel. In response, the people cried despondently, and as a result, the gift of the Land of Israel was taken away from them; they were denied entry.

2) The First Temple was destroyed.

3) The Second Temple was destroyed.

4) The Romans, a few years later, crushed the Bar Kochva revolt. This was a movement to regain sovereignty in the Land, rebuild the Temple and reclaim self-rule. The decisive end of this movement and dream came with the bloody destruction of the city of Beitar on the 9th of Av.

5) Following the crushing defeat of the Bar Kochva revolt, the Roman commander Turnus Rufus plowed the site of the Temple in Jerusalem and the surrounding area.

Before going deeper, it is important to reiterate two fundamental points: 1) These are not random events that coincidentally happened to have occurred on the same day; and 2) the first of each of the above sets of five events is the root of the other four. The deep error of the Meraglim, and the senseless weeping that followed, is the reason that both Temples were destroyed, the dream of rebuilding the Temple was crushed and the site of the destroyed Temple was desecrated.

Let's now explore the deeper meanings of these events: Why exactly is the Golden Calf and the breaking of the Luchos the beginning of Bein haMetzarim and the 'three weeks', and what makes Tisha b'Av a fitting conclusion to this process?

The answer is: there is a 'Plan A', a 'Plan B' and a 'Plan C' for Creation.

Plan A:
Connecting to the Transcendent Beyond All Images

After Matan Torah, when Hashem revealed, "I am your G-d", it was deeply understood by all that Hashem's Presence is everywhere, while also being beyond any particular image. Hashem also announced to the People of Israel, "An altar of earth you shall make for Me, and you shall slaughter beside it your burnt offerings and your peace offerings, your sheep and your cattle. Wherever My name is mentioned, I will come to you and bless you" (*Shemos*, 20:21). This means that from the elevated perspective of Matan Torah, we do not need a particular place to connect with Hashem, as indeed Hashem is everywhere. In this state, any place is appropriate for gathering some earth and making an altar to the Divine. Hashem is Infinite, with no location or limitation, and gives life to all life; we can therefore connect to Hashem, and be fully alive, in any location (*Meshech Chochmah*, ad loc).

This is the vision of a perfect world, a place where we *live with* the Omnipresent One, not merely 'believe in monotheism'. Klal Yisrael, however, proved that they were not yet on that level of perfection — they were not yet spiritually mature enough to live in a relationship with Hashem without any defined locations or 'images'. Thus, when the image of Moshe was no longer with them, and it appeared that he would not return from the top of Mount Sinai, they asked Aaron to create an intermediary 'image' for them. Perhaps they naively thought that it would be an innocent 'replacement' for Moshe's image. In any case, they felt that they needed some kind of image to help them connect with the Imageless One, and so they sought to create a Golden Calf. The People came before Aaron and told him, "Make us an *Elokim* because the man Moshe — we don't know what happened to him." In this sentence, *Elokim* does not necessarily mean a 'god', but rather a powerful leadership figure. They were saying, 'We know that Hashem is Transcendent, beyond all image-ing and imagining, but we can only relate to the Transcendent Leader of All via Moshe, the tangible, visible leader of our people.' They were accustomed to having a tangible presence, Moshe, as a focus and access point when they were seeking to connect to Hashem, the 'intangible' *Ein Sof* / Infinite One.

They wanted, as the Even Ezra writes, "the glory (of Hashem) to be incarnate, in a physical form". Similarly, in the words of the Kuzari, Rabbi Yehudah HaLevi states: "They wanted to always have a *Muchash* / a tangible aspect to worship" (*Kuzari*, Ma'amar 1, 91-117).

When Moshe came down from the Mountain with the Luchos and saw the people dancing around the Golden Calf, he assessed their collective state of consciousness and inferred that they would also most likely idolize the objects in his hands. They would merely substitute the image of the Golden Calf for the image of the Luchos, just as they had substituted the image of the Golden Calf for Moshe himself. They would not be able to focus on the spiritual meaning of the writing on the Luchos, but only on the physical forms of the Luchos themselves. Therefore, Moshe smashed the most sacred artifacts of Torah, the handiwork of Hashem, the holy 'First Luchos'. This dramatic moment effectively ended Hashem's initial Plan A for the Jewish People and for the world.

If it were not for this spiritual descent, we would have received the First Luchos in their perfect, unbroken form. As a result, we, too, would have been 'unbroken', and we would have remained at the integrally elevated level of Sinai for perpetuity — the world would then have been free of death, separation, forgetfulness, destruction and exile (see; *Medrash Rabbah*, Shemos, 41:7. *Eiruvin*, 54a). We would have been able to connect to the Infinite One in any place, at any time, with or without the presence of tangible images. Perhaps there would have been no reason at all for the Mishkan, according to Rashi (who views the Mishkan primarily as a place of atonement for the Golden Calf). Certainly in an unbroken, redeemed world, there would be no foreign occupation of holy places, nor any 'breaching' of the walls protecting them. There would, in effect, be no 'lack' for anyone, anywhere, ever.

However, the People of Israel were not ready for the quantum leap of consciousness required by 'Plan A'. And because of this inability, which resulted in the Golden Calf, Hashem's 'Plan B' for Creation came into play.

Plan B:
Connecting to the Transcendent through a Divinely Chosen Place

After the people were forgiven for the *Cheit haEgel* / error of the Golden Calf, Hashem told Moshe to transmit the Mitzvah of constructing the Mishkan to them: "And you shall make for me a Mikdash". This Mitzvah also included within it the eventual building of the Temple of stone in Yerushalayim. As the Rambam writes, "It is a positive commandment to construct a House for Hashem..., as [*Shemos*, 25:8] states: 'And you shall make Me a sanctuary.' The sanctuary constructed by Moshe [in the Desert]...was only temporary, as [*Devarim*, 12:9] states: 'For at present, you have not come unto [the resting place and the inheritance of] Yerushalayim.'"[*Zevachim*, 119a)] (*Hilchos Beis haBechirah*, 1:1).

Building a specific space to connect with the Divine was thus 'Plan B', which implied that there should be an actual physical structure containing Divinely prescribed 'images' such as the *Keruvim* (See *Medrash Rabbah*, Eichah, Pesicha), and that Kedusha would flow from the Transcendent through this location.

In a way, the Mishkan was thus a Divine concession. Following the episode of the Golden Calf, Hashem was saying to the Israelites: 'Okay, if you really need an image to connect with Me, make this specific structure, containing these specific objects and images, but you must always remember that its one and only purpose is to connect with Me *beyond* the image.' Hashem then chose a specific location and focal point through which we could feel connected with Transcendence:

"These are the statutes and ordinances that you shall keep to perform in the Land...: You shall utterly destroy all the places where the nations, that you shall possess, worshipped idols..., and then, Hashem your G-d shall choose a portion of land from all your tribes, to set His Name there.... And it will be, that the place Hashem will choose in which to establish His Name, there you shall bring all that I am commanding you: your burnt offerings, and your sacrifices" (*Devarim*, 12:1-11).

From the above passage, it is clear that 'Plan B' included not only the construction of a permanent Beis haMikdash in a precise location in Yerushalayim, but also then serving the Infinite One in a prescribed way there, until the time was ripe for the coming of Moshiach. But, as discussed previously, the Meraglim did not want to go into the Land, and therefore, because of them, neither did the people. In fact, they wept bitterly, thinking it was impossible to settle the Land. As a consequence, even after the next generation did finally enter the Land, it was not to be permanent. The 'images' of the Temples were destroyed and we were exiled, in accordance with our very desire to not enter in the first place.

The people in the Desert who created the Golden Calf were the same people who did not desire to enter the Land of Israel on account of the Meraglim's negative report. They wanted a fixed image to worship, proven by the fact that they created the Golden Calf in Moshe's absence, but they also wanted a type of freedom to roam in the desert where they could continue to live nomadically and not settle in a 'serious' land with all the attendant responsibilities of self-rule that comes along with such an enterprise. They could accept a Mishkan in the desert, as it, too, would move about as they continued their journey through the desert; they just did not want to settle in a particular, permanent location.

As a consequence of our initial desires, even after we collectively entered into the land, although it was meant to be permanent, the Temples were eventually destroyed and we were exiled and had to live as diasporic nomads — roaming indeterminately throughout the nations of the world.

The episode of the Meraglim is thus the root cause of the destructions of both Temples, and all the exiles from the Land of Israel that followed. It is also the cause of the exile that we are still living in today, despite the valiant attempts of many to attain Redemption, such as Bar Kochva and his revolt.*

All our exiles are thus rooted in the story of the Meraglim, as the verses in Tehilim (Psalms) say clearly: "Then they despised the

---

*In this way, the 17th of Tamuz is connected to the unfulfilled objective of Matan Torah, and the 9th of Av is connected to the unfulfilled objective of entering the Land of Israel. "There were no greater days than Tu b'Av and Yom Kippur." Correspondingly, Tu b'Av is connected to entering into the land, as it was the day when the Generation of the Desert stopped dying; and Yom Kippur is connected to Matan Torah, as it is the day we received the second set of Luchos.

pleasant land; they did not believe his promise...So He swore...He would make them fall in the wilderness, make their descendants fall among the nations and scatter them throughout the lands"(*Tehilim*, 106:24-27). The scattering throughout the lands is caused by the story of the Meraglim, where they despised the land and did not believe that the Land of Israel was a good and habitable land.

'Plan B' was thus not viable, and so 'Plan C' came into focus. We are still living out this third part of the story to this very day.

Plan C:
Sifting Through the Shards

In 'Plan C', it is revealed that there is in fact a purpose behind the many years of exile, despite the terrible sufferings involved. "The reason Klal Yisrael was exiled among the nations of the world was so converts would be added to them" (*Pesachim* 87b). 'Adding converts', on a deeper level, means sifting through and refining the material dimensions of this world in order to find and elevate the sparks of holiness that are dispersed there (Shaloh, *Torah Ohr*, Matos –Maasei. R. Tzadok of Lublin, *Resisei Layla*, 57). We are now tasked with elevating all the elements of 'image' and 'location' within Creation back to the imageless, locationless Creator. We accomplish this through performing Mitzvos according to the 'broken' Tablets, the Torah that shines even within the ruins of exile. In this way, we will be able to reveal Hashem's presence everywhere, no matter how broken or low, thereby coming to realize that we are always at home, even in exile. For, truly, "If I ascend to the heights, you are there; and even if I make my bed in the depths, you are also there" (*Tehilim* 139:8).

When this long, complex and holy task has finally been completed, we will recover the scattered sparks of 'Plan B' and even 'Plan A'.

The Temple in Yerushalayim will be rebuilt, *and* we will be able to connect with the Omnipresent in every place, with or without any 'image'. May it happen soon and in our days!

OTHER BOOKS BY THE AUTHOR

RECLAIMING THE SELF
The Way of Teshuvah

Teshuvah is one of the great gifts of life. It speaks of a hope for a better today and empowers us to choose a brighter tomorrow. But what exactly is Teshuvah? How does it work? How can we undo our past and how do we deal with guilt? And what is healthy regret without eroding our self-esteem? In this fascinating and empowering book, the path for genuine transformation and a way to include all of our past in the powerful moment of the now, is explored and demonstrated.

THE MYSTERY OF KADDISH
Understanding the Mourner's Kaddish

The Mystery of Kaddish is an in-depth exploration into the Mourner's Prayer. Throughout Jewish history, there have been many rites and rituals associated with loss and mourning, yet none have prevailed quite like the Mourner's Kaddish Prayer, which has become the definitive ritual of mourning. The book explores the source of this prayer and deconstructs the meaning to better understand the grieving process and how the Kaddish prayer supports and uplifts the bereaved through their own personal journey to healing.

UPSHERNISH: THE FIRST HAIRCUT
Exploring the Laws, Customs & Meanings of a Boy's First Haircut

What is the meaning of Upsherin, the traditional celebration of a boy's first haircut at the age of three? Why is a boy's hair allowed to grow freely for his first three years? What is the deeper import of hair in all its lengths and varieties? What is the meaning of hair coverings? Includes a guide to conducting an Upsherin ceremony.

A BOND FOR ETERNITY
Understanding the Bris Milah

What is the Bris Milah – the covenant of circumcision? What does it represent, symbolize and signify? This book provides an in depth and sensitive review of this fundamental Mitzvah. In this little masterpiece of wisdom – profound yet accessible —the deeper meaning of this essential rite of passage and its eternal link to the Jewish people, is revealed and explored.

REINCARNATION AND JUDAISM
The Journey of the Soul

A fascinating analysis of the concept of Gilgul / Reincarnation. Dipping into the fountain of ancient wisdom and modern understanding, this book addresses and answers such basic questions as: What is reincarnation? Why does it occur? And how does it affect us personally?

INNER RHYTHMS
The Kabbalah of MUSIC

Exploring the inner dimension of sound and music, and particularly, how music permeates all aspects of life. The topics range from Deveikus/Unity and Yichudim/Unifications, to the more personal issues, such as Simcha/Happiness and Marirus/ sadness.

MEDITATION AND JUDAISM
Exploring the Jewish Meditative Paths

A comprehensive work encompassing the entire spectrum of Jewish thought, from the sages of the Talmud and the early Kabbalists to the modern philosophers and Chassidic masters. This book is both a scholarly, in-depth study of meditative practices, and a practical, easy to follow guide for any person interested in meditating the Jewish way.

TOWARD THE INFINITE

A book focusing exclusively on the Chassidic approach to meditation known as Hisbonenus. Encompassing the entire meditative experience, it takes the reader on a comprehensive and engaging journey through this unique practice. The book explores the various states of consciousness that a person encounters in the course of the meditation, beginning at a level of extreme self-awareness and concluding with a state of total non-awareness.

THIRTY – TWO GATES OF WISDOM
Awakening through Kabbalah

Kabbalah holds the secrets to a path of conscious awareness. In this compact book, 32 key concepts of Kabbalah are explored and their value in opening the gates of perception are demonstrated.

THE PURIM READER
The Holiday of Purim Explored

With a Persian name, a masquerade dress code and a woman as the heroine, Purim is certainly unusual amongst the Jewish holidays. Most people are very familiar with the costumes, Megilah and revelry, but are mystified by their significance. This book offers a glimpse into the hidden world of Purim, uncovering these mysteries and offering a deeper understanding of this unique holiday.

EIGHT LIGHTS
8 Meditations for Chanukah

What is the meaning and message of Chanukah? What is the spiritual significance of the Lights of the Menorah? What are the Lights telling us? What is the deeper dimension of the Dreidel? Rav Pinson, with his trademark deep learning and spiritual sensitivity guides us through eight meditations relating to the Lights of the Menorah, the eight days of Chanukah, and a fascinating exploration of the symbolism and structure of the Dreidel. Includes a detailed how-to guide for lighting the Chanukah Menorah.

THE IYYUN HAGADAH
An Introduction to the Haggadah

In this beautifully written introduction to Passover and the Haggadah, we are guided through the major themes of Passover and the Seder night. This slim text, addresses the important questions, such as: What is the big deal of Chametz? What are we trying to achieve through conducting a Seder? What's with all that stuff on the Seder Plate? And most importantly, how is this all related to freedom?

PASSPORT TO KABBALAH
A Journey of Inner Transformation

Life is a journey full of ups and downs, inside-outs, and unexpected detours. There are times when we think we know exactly where we want to be headed, and other times when we are so lost we don't even know where we are. This slim book provides readers with a passport of sorts to help them through any obstacles along their path of self-refinement, reflection, and self-transformation.

THE FOUR SPECIES
The Symbolism of the Lulav & Esrog

The Four Species have inspired countless commentaries and traditions and intrigued scholars and mystics alike. In this little masterpiece of wisdom both profound and practical - the deep symbolic roots and nature of the Four Species are explored. The Na'anuim, or ritual of the Lulav movement, is meticulously detailed and Kavanos,, are offered for use with the practice. Includes an illustrated guide to the Lulav Movements.

THE BOOK OF LIFE AFTER LIFE

What is a soul? What happens to us after we physically die?

What is consciousness, and can it survive without a physical brain?

Can we remember our past lives?

Do near-death experiences prove immortality?

What is Gan Eden? Resurrection?

Exploring the possibility of surviving death, the near-death experience and a glimpse into what awaits us after this life.

(This book is an updated and expanded version of the book; Jewish Wisdom of the Afterlife)

THE GARDEN OF PARADOX:
The Essence of Non - Dual Kabbalah

This book is a Primer on the Essential Philosophy of Kabbalah presented as a series of 3 conversations, revealing the mysteries of Creator, Creation and Consciousness. With three representational students, embodying respectively, the philosopher, the activist and the mystic, the book, tackles the larger questions of life. Who is G-d? Who am I? Why do I exist? What is my purpose in this life? Written in clear and concise prose, the text, gently guides the reader towards making sense of life's paradoxes and living meaningfully.

BREATHING & QUIETING THE MIND

Achieving a sense of self-mastery and inner freedom demands that we gain a measure of hegemony over our thoughts. We learn to choose out thoughts so that we are not at the mercy of whatever belches up to the mind. Through quieting the mind and conscious breathing we can slow the onrush of anxious, scattered thinking and come to a deeper awareness of the interconnectedness of all of life.

Source texts are included in translation, with how-to-guides for the various practices.

VISUALIZATION AND IMAGERY:
Harnessing the Power of our Mind's Eye

We assume that what we see with our eyes is absolute. Yet, beyond our ability to choose what we see, we have the ability to choose how we see. This directly translates into how we experience life. In a world saturated with visual imagery, our senses are continuously assaulted with Kelipa/empty/fantasy imagery that we would not necessarily choose. These images can negatively affect our relationship with ourselves, with the world around us, and with the Divine. This volume seeks to show us how we can alter that which we observe through harnessing the power of our mind's eye, the inner sanctum of our imagination. We thus create a new way to see and experience the world. This book teaches us how to utilize visualization and imagery as a way to develop our spiritual sensitivity and higher intuition, and ultimately achieve Deveikus/Unity with Hashem.

THE POWER OF CHOICE:
A Practical Guide to Conscious Living

It is the essential premise of this book that we hold the key to unlock many of the gates that seem closed to us and keep us from living our fullest life. That key we all hold is the power to choose. The Power of Choice is the primary tool that we have at our disposal to impact the world and effect change within our own lives. We often give up this power to outside forces such as the market, media, politicians or peer pressure; or to internal forces that often function beyond our conscious control such as ego, anger, lust, greed or jealousy. Making conscious, compassionate and creative decisions is the cornerstone of living a mature and meaningful life.

MYSTIC TALES FROM THE EMEK HAMELECH

Mystic Tales of the Emek HaMelech, is a wondrous and inspiring collection of stories culled from the Emek HaMelech. Emek HaMelech, from which these stories have been taken, (as well as its author) is a bit of a mystery. But like all good mysteries, it is one worth investigating. In this spirit the present volume is being offered to the general public in the merit and memory of its saintly author, as well as in the hopes of introducing a vital voice of deeper Torah teaching and tradition to a contemporary English speaking audience

---

INNER WORLDS OF JEWISH PRAYER
A Guide to Develop and Deepen the Prayer Experience

While much attention has been paid to the poetry, history, theology and contextual meaning of the prayers, the intention of this work is to provide a guide to finding meaning and effecting transformation through the prayer experience itself.

Explore: *What happens when we pray? *How do we enter the mind-state of prayer? *Learning to incorporate the body into the prayers. *Discover techniques to enhance and deepen prayer and make it a transformative experience.

This empowering and inspiring text, demonstrates how through proper mindset, preparation and dedication, the experience of prayer can be deeply transformative and ultimately, life-altering.

WRAPPED IN MAJESTY
Tefillin – Exploring the Mystery

Tefillin, the black boxes and leather straps that are worn during prayer, are curiously powerful and mysterious. Within the inky black boxes lie untold secrets. In this profound, passionate and thought-provoking text, the multi-dimensional perspectives of Tefillin are explored and revealed. Magically weaving together all levels of Torah including the Peshat (literal observation), to Remez (allegorical), to Derush, (homiletic), to Sod (hidden) into one beautiful tapestry. Inspirational and instructive, Wrapped in Majesty: Tefillin, will make putting on the Tefillin more meaningful and inspiring.

THE SPIRAL OF TIME:
A 12 Part Series on the Months of the Year.

NOW AVAILABLE!

THE SPIRAL OF TIME:
Unraveling the Yearly Cycle

Many centuries ago, the Sages of Israel were the foremost authority in the fields of both astronomical calculation and astrological wisdom, including the deeper interpretations of the cycles and seasons. Over time, this wisdom became hidden within the esoteric teachings of the Torah, and as a result was known only to students and scholars of the deepest depths of the tradition. More recently, the great teachers, from R.Yitzchak Luria (the Arizal) to the Baal Shem Tov, taught that as the world approaches the Era of Redemption, it is a Mitzvah / spiritual obligation to broadly reveal this wisdom.

"The Spiral of Time" is volume 1 is a series of 12 books, and serves as an introductory book to the basic concepts and nature of the Hebrew calendar and explores the special day of Rosh Chodesh.

THE MONTH OF SHEVAT: ELEVATING EATING
& The Holiday of Tu b'Shevat

Each month of the year radiates with a distinct Divine energy and thus unique opportunities for growth, *Tikkun* and illumination. According to the deeper teachings of the Torah, all of these distinct qualities, opportunities and natural phenomena correspond to a certain data set. That is, the nature of each month is elucidated by a specific letter of the Aleph Beis, a tribe, verse, human sense, and so forth. The month of Shevat is particularly connected to food and our relationship to bodily intake. During this month we celebrate Tu b'Shevat, the New Year of the Tree, and aspire to create a proper and physically/emotionally/spiritually healthy relationship with food.

THE MONTH OF IYYAR: EVOLVING THE SELF
& The Holiday of LAG B'OMER

The month of IYYAR is the second month of the spring, a month that connects the Redemption from Egypt in Nissan with the Revelation of Torah in Sivan. The Chai/ Eighteenth day of the

Month is the day we celebrate the Rashbi (Rabbi Shimon Bar Yo-chai) and the revealing of the hidden aspects of the Torah. This is the 'Holiday' of Lag b'Omer. The book explores the unique quality of this special month, a month that has a Mitzvah of counting the Omer every day. In addition, the book explores the roots and significance of the mystical 'holiday' of Lag b'Omer. Including the customs & Practices of Lag b'Omer, such as, bonfires, bows & arrows, parades, Upsherin, and more.

www.ingramcontent.com/pod-product-compliance
Lightning Source LLC
Chambersburg PA
CBHW060756100426
42813CB00004B/837